I0820542

a
witch
is...

About the Author

Raechel Henderson is a Pagan and a witch, following an eclectic and independent path. She currently works with Hestia and Turtle in her magical practice. She contributes articles to Llewellyn's almanacs and calendars, and she blogs about magic, creativity, and living by your own patterns. Raechel is a dual-class seamstress/shieldmaiden and has been sewing professionally since 2008. She is also the author of *Sew Witchy*, *The Scent of Lemon & Rosemary*, *The Natural Home Wheel of the Year*, and *The Witch's Wardrobe*. Visit her on Instagram: @idiorhythmic.

a witch is...

13 Keys to Witchcraft

RAECHEL HENDERSON

WOODBURY, MINNESOTA

First Edition
First Printing, 2026

Cover design by Shira Atakpu

Library of Congress Cataloging-in-Publication Data (Pending)
ISBN: 978-0-7387-8125-9

Llewellyn Publications
A Division of Llewellyn Worldwide Ltd.
2143 Wooddale Drive
Woodbury, MN 55125-2989
www.llewellyn.com

Printed in the United States of America

GPSR Representation:
UPI-2M PLUS d.o.o., Medulićeva 20, 10000 Zagreb, Croatia
matt.parsons@upi2mbooks.hr

Also by Raechel Henderson

Magic Month by Month

The Natural Home Wheel of the Year

The Scent of Lemon & Rosemary

Sew Witchy

The Witch's Wardrobe

Yulecraft

Dedication

Dedicated to all the witches who have come before me and who have passed on their knowledge to those who followed.

Contents

Introduction

I've been a witch all my life. I knew I was a witch when I was a child. Growing up going to the First Baptist Church taught me to keep my identity to myself. But even when I was at my most devout, I still felt the pull to the magical. When I reached adulthood, I discovered Wicca, and though I never identified as such, the discovery opened up a whole new world of magic and witchcraft to me. It was a world in which others cast spells, divined fortunes, and called themselves witches without shame or embarrassment. I wish I could say that I embraced that openness back then. Instead, the everyday struggles of living—school, work, keeping house, and so on—all conspired to fill my days so that I didn't have time to devote to my craft. More importantly, I was in a relationship with someone who actively worked to make me small and powerless. Once again I hid my light, keeping any thoughts of magic or being a witch to myself.

It wasn't until 2008 that I finally broke free and threw off all the layers of "normalcy" that I had hidden under for so many years. That year I got divorced, started a sewing business, and returned to my practice. Ever since then, I have refused to go back into the "broom closet."

A Witch Is is a compilation of all the lessons I have learned during both my undercover and my out-and-proud years of being a witch. They are fundamental to practicing witchcraft in a way that not only is effective but also aligns with one's personal ethics. One thing I've learned is that there are as many ways of practicing magic as there are witches. What might work for others might not work for you. This is because magic is personal. Knowing that, I wrote this book to give you a guide on how to create your own, individual vision of what it means to be a witch.

My goal with *A Witch Is* is to provide you with a different perspective when it comes to magic and witchcraft. You won't find tables of correspondences here. Instead, you'll create your own. You will be encouraged to think about what living a magical life means to you. And while there are a few spells included in the book, you'll be challenged to go beyond the basics and create your own spells and rituals. It is my hope that by the end of this book, you will have a dozen new tools at your disposal to take your magic further.

While each chapter focuses on a specific lesson, many of them are interconnected. Several of the exercises build on those that come before or refer back to previous ones. As such, I recommend reading the book from start to finish, rather than jumping around. You might want to journal along as you read, highlight passages, write notes in the margin, or bookmark places that resonate with you. I encourage that. Treat this like a workbook if it helps you become a better witch.

Treat this like a workbook if it helps you become a better witch.

At the end of the book, you'll find a list of recommended reading. These are books that influenced my own magical journey, and that I hope you'll find useful as well. I encourage you to not only read other books on witchcraft and magic but also follow the authors on social media. Platforms like Bluesky and Instagram are seeing a depth and breadth of conversations regarding magic that will only improve your practice.

Magical Terms

Throughout the book, you'll find me using certain terms and phrases. These include terms like *materia magica* and *book of shadows*. An explanation of these terms follows.

Materia Magic

Materia magica is simply a fancy name for spell components. Every ingredient you use in magic is materia magica, from herbs to crystals to moon water to soil. I use this term because it makes me feel more magical and witchy. While much of magic is about substance, the rest is about style, and sometimes I need that little boost. I also like to use the term because many of the components I use for spells come from my kitchen cupboard. Calling my bay leaves materia magica when I use them in spellwork helps me shift from thinking of them as mundane to magical.

Book of Shadows

A book of shadows is a book that some witches keep. They might keep notes on spells, lists of correspondences, information on various herbs, crystals, magical timing, and so on. It is part journal, part log, and part textbook.[1] I don't have a personal book of shadows, but instead I keep a journal for each year in which I write

1. For more information on books of shadows, see *The Witch's Book of Shadows: The Craft, Lore & Magick of the Witch's Grimoire* by Jason Mankey.

down what I'm working on, what the results are, and how I might improve my spellcasting in the future.

Genius Loci

This is a term that means "spirit of the place" and refers to those spirits that reside in a certain place. These can be found in large areas like parks and forests or in smaller spaces like stones and trees. There will be places in *A Witch Is* that will have you connect with the genius loci of areas near where you live. They can be powerful allies in your magic.

Magical Skills

There are certain skills you'll need to practice in order to get the most results from your magic. Not only do these form the foundation of magical practice, but they will help you advance to higher levels of spellcasting once you've mastered them. In this section, we'll discuss two main techniques: centering and grounding.

Centering

To be centered is to know what is going on with your body, both physically and magically. It is to be comfortable in yourself, to know your boundaries, and to be able to work with forces outside of yourself with less risk.[2] Centering also brings you to a calm state from which to work, keeping your emotions and any intrusive thoughts from interfering with your magical work.

Centering yourself is both simple and difficult. On the surface, all it requires is for you to become aware of your breathing and your physical body. You bring your attention to parts of your body,

2. There is always risk when working with magical forces, but centering will help mitigate it.

letting all thoughts go and letting your breathing come naturally. This is easier said than done, especially in the beginning, and also if you have conditions like ADHD that might make it difficult to concentrate. My advice is to start small and practice the technique several times throughout the day. If you do so, you'll soon find that you can center yourself within a second or two on command.

To start, close your eyes. Doing so helps cut down on outside distractions. Bring your attention to your breathing, inhaling and exhaling at an easy pace. Keep your attention on your breath for three to five inhalations. Then bring your attention to your chest or stomach, whichever you view as the center of your body. Feel your body around you: your toes, your fingers, knees, shoulders, head, and center. Remind yourself that this is your body; you occupy this space. What does it feel like to be in your body and aware of it? You may feel some tingling in your fingers or hands or even at the back of your neck. This is normal. Remember what this feels like so that you can more easily reach a centered state in the future. Breathe for another three to five inhalations and then bring your awareness back to the world around you. Open your eyes.

Practice the centering technique several times a day until you can center yourself just by thinking about it. Knowing where your body starts and ends and what it feels like to be in it will aid you before you cast a spell, as it will help you focus on the steps and your goals, and it will help you should you decide to work with deities or spirits. Being centered will allow you to know when you are encountering the thoughts and desires of something that is outside of yourself. This means that you will better be able to determine if the communication coming to you from a spirit or deity is real or just a manifestation of your own mind and desires.

Grounding

Grounding is a technique that allows you to exchange energy with the ground, thus the name. You can send any negative or unhelpful emotions, energy, or thoughts into the earth. On the flip side, you can draw up positive, uplifting energy from the earth to fill you up. Grounding is another technique that is easy enough to do, but requires a bit of practice to get the hang of it. Ideally, you would ground outside on the earth with bare feet. I recommend doing so whenever you can, as it is the most beneficial way to ground yourself. However, you can do so inside with shoes on by utilizing your imagination.

To start, stand with your feet firmly planted on the ground. You can close your eyes if you wish to block out any distractions. Take a deep breath in, and on the exhale, visualize roots coming out of the bottom of your feet and burrowing into the earth. If you are inside, imagine those roots digging through the carpet or hardwood floor you are standing on into rich, dark earth underneath. If you aren't a visually inclined person, you can instead feel the roots going from your feet into the ground. Once you are rooted, imagine any negative energy, any tension, any unhelpful thoughts or feelings leaving your body through those roots and entering the earth. It may help to push those things out on your exhalations. See all that negativity and everything that doesn't serve you being taken in by the earth and turned into positive and nurturing energy, in just the same way that dead leaves and branches are broken down into compost on the forest floor.

Now that you are empty, see your roots drawing up good, helpful energy from the earth. Feel that positivity filling your entire body, from the tips of your toes to the top of your head. You may visualize this energy as white or blue or green light. It might feel like warmth, or have a sensation of tingling. However you experience it, know that you are being refilled by the earth with nurturing energy to help you fulfill your purpose. Once you feel full, visualize your roots retracting back into your feet, severing your connection with the earth for now.

You can pair grounding with centering to give you a magical energetic boost at any time, day or night. Ground before you perform magic, before you have your big presentation at work, when you aren't feeling great, or whenever you feel like you could use a magical refresh.

How to Do the Exercises

At the end of each chapter in *A Witch Is*, you will find exercises to do. Many will require you to do some sort of writing. You can use a journal dedicated to this activity, your book of shadows (if you keep one), sheets of paper, or even the Notes app on your phone if you so choose. The important thing is to write down your answers to the questions in each exercise. Writing helps aid in memory retention and understanding. Also, several of the exercises will call back to earlier ones, so you will want to have those notes on hand as you go through the book.

Set aside some quiet time to do each exercise. About a half hour will give you time to settle down, prepare yourself, and write. However, take as much time as you need to write down everything that comes to mind. When you are going through the exercises, try to limit distractions: silence your phone; make sure you won't be interrupted by family, friends, or pets; and turn off any noise if it will keep you from focusing. You might, however, like to put on a little music if that will help you relax.

Writing helps aid in memory retention and understanding.

You can make each exercise a ritual by lighting incense and candles. If you choose to use an incense, I recommend lavender or rosemary, as both help relax and calm the mind. Before beginning, sit and center yourself, and then take a few deep breaths. Then read through the exercise and begin writing. Work until you feel you have hit a natural stopping point. While you are writing, don't edit or censor your thoughts. No one other than yourself will see these notes unless you decide to share them. Just write until the words no longer come to you. At that point, you can spend a few minutes grounding yourself and any emotions the writing brought up.

If you aren't a writer, you can also use other methods to work through the exercises. You can draw your answers, use techniques such as mind maps, or even create collages. The point is to find the method that works for you and that you relate to. Each exercise is meant to delve into your individual approach to magic and witchcraft, so the way you engage in them should be personal to you.

Once you are finished with the exercise, you can put your work away for a day or two and then return to it with fresh eyes. This allows your answers time to marinate in the back of your mind. You might find that your initial response to the questions has changed, or you might want to expand on what you answered. Return to your answers as often as you want to adjust, edit, add to them, or just reflect on them. These are the blueprint to your approach to your craft.

A Witch Is Resourceful

Resourcefulness is our birthright. Until the late eighteenth century, most of our ancestors had to make do with what they had on hand. They built, sewed, and baked what they needed. And when they didn't have the exact ingredient or material to accomplish a task, they came up with a substitution or work-around. Even after the rise of capitalism, bringing with it factory-made goods and department stores, you find the make-do spirit during Depression-era America with flour sack dresses and eggless cakes. There is a similar attitude alive today, with the underconsumption and mending movements seeing people looking to the past for ways to extend the lives of their possessions.

This resourcefulness has been especially present in magic. Before there was online shopping and two-day shipping, witches worked with what they could find or make. Take, for example, candles and candle magic. Until the early 1800s, candles were expensive and smelly items. They were made of animal fat or beeswax, with some cultures using even more exotic materials, such as fish, to light the darkness. It wasn't until the development of paraffin wax in 1830 that candles became cheap and readily available. Candles weren't colored until the invention of paraffin wax, and once they were, the practice of candle magic exploded, fueled by hoodoo practice and books such as *The Master Book of Candle-Burning.*[3] Prior to this advancement in candlemaking, candle magic didn't really have a color component, as candles weren't dyed. Witches saw the usefulness of bringing color magic into their practice through candles, and a whole new branch of witchcraft was born, was expanded upon, and flourished in the following years.

One only has to look at the magical properties of herbs to see more resourcefulness in action. In *Cunningham's Encyclopedia of Magical Herbs*, 149 herbs that have magical properties of attracting love are listed. That number contains plants from all over the world, indicating how many people scoured their environment for an appropriate materia magica rather than importing an exotic herb. The same goes for crystals and metals. The natural world provides us with what we need for our magic. We just have to know where, and how, to look.

This is why the lesson of resourcefulness is the first we'll tackle. It is a skill that has naturally declined over the last couple of centuries. This is especially true for witches and witchcraft. Both have been embraced by mainstream audiences, leading to access to a wider range of magical accoutrements, fashion, home decor, and materia magica. This has been a boon to witches who might have had a hard time getting certain items otherwise—with a click of a button, they can find thousands of witchy products online. It has also allowed those who would otherwise not be able to express

3. "How to Practice Hoodoo Candle Magic," catherine yronwode, accessed November 21, 2024, https://www.luckymojo.com/candlemagic.html.

their magical selves a cover through "spooky" and "quirky" witchy designs. Is the person wearing a "Live, Laugh, Hex" t-shirt a witch or just someone with a sense of humor? Who knows?

This widespread acceptance of magic and witchcraft has its downside as well. The rise in corporations rushing to tap into the market means that conscientious witches have to be prepared to evaluate everything they buy. Is it ethically sourced? Has it been appropriated from a culture that was, or perhaps even still is, prohibited from using it? What are the working conditions in which it was created? Is it from a small creator or a large corporation? That's a lot to have to consider when you're looking at a selenite orb for your crystal collection. Which brings us back to resourcefulness. When you are able to look past the low-hanging fruit of the Halloween section of your local craft store, you can make decisions that align with your ethics and make you feel good about your purchases, when you do make them.

So what is resourcefulness, and how can you make it work for you as a witch? Simply, resourcefulness means finding ways to overcome obstacles. In the case of witchcraft, that involves finding ways to cast magic even when you don't have all the "right" equipment. While it is true that intention is all you need for magic, materia magica, tools, garb, and other aesthetic and theatrical items help you sharpen your intention and narrow your focus for better spellcasting results. Frugality, reusing items, and some good old-fashioned creative thinking are all cornerstones of resourcefulness. We'll go through these in the following section, and there will be two exercises at the end of this chapter to get you started in building your resourcefulness muscles.

But before we move on, let me give you an example of resourcefulness from my own life. In 2022, my family and I moved several states away from Illinois to Wyoming. We could only take what we could pack into a small trailer, which meant we left a good chunk of our possessions behind. This included my well-stocked apothecary, which I had built up over four years and which included several items that were used to process various herbs and plant material. I got to Wyoming and our new home bereft of the familiar jars and bags and boxes of materia magica. I wasn't long without, however, as my cousin started funneling some of the bounty of her own garden my way. I was soon inundated with sunflowers and peppermint as a witchy housewarming gift.

See where you could fit in magic in places you haven't before.

The problem was that I had nowhere to hang up these fragrant bouquets. We were still unpacking and strapped for cash after the move. So I did what I've always done and looked at what we had on hand: a ball of twine, clothespins, and two door-stops that we had removed from the floors of the new house. I climbed up on the counter in the kitchen and installed the door-stops over one of the windows. I then strung the twine between them and hung the bundles of herbs and flowers from the twine with the clothespins. Is it an elegant and beautiful solution? No. But is it practical and does it work? Yes. Two years on, my ad hoc herb-drying line still works.

I encourage you, as you go through the rest of the chapter, to look around your home and life and see where you could fit in magic in places you haven't before. Look at your bedroom, on your bookshelves, inside your fridge and closet and consider how little space there is between the mundane and the magical.

Thinking Differently

As I mentioned earlier, resourcefulness encompasses two different skills or mindsets: frugality and reusing items, both of which fuel creative thinking. These two might not sound witchy at all. They might even sound boring. But frugality and reusing items are peak witchcraft. They involve looking at items and situations with new eyes. And what is witchcraft if not seeing, and thinking, differently?

Frugality

Being frugal doesn't mean being cheap, but it does mean being mindful of your expenditures. Living in a capitalist society underscores the idea that money can bring power. We want to harness that power to our advantage both physically and magically. Even when we have little of it to begin with, we can work the system into our witchcraft to subvert it to our will. This encompasses not only money magic but also pushing back against the consumerism that is thrust on us twenty-four hours a day, seven days a week.

The underconsumption and minimalism movements that have gained popularity over the past decade point to a way to slow down our mindless consumption. By taking that break, we reclaim power from a society that pushes us to collect more and more, all in the name of GDP and consumer confidence. Capitalism tells us that we must spend money to live. Thrifting, repairing, and taking time to consider all options before hitting the "buy" button wrests control back. And through that control, we can make sure that when we do spend our money, we are buying the right item that will suit our magical needs perfectly.

Tapping into your frugality can help you connect with your ancestors. Scores of people who counted their pennies, spent their money wisely, and made sure they got a good value for their hard-earned money are watching you, with your access to a nearly unlimited variety of goods and services. They are urging you on with their wisdom. I have, oftentimes, invoked my great-grandmother in my purchasing decisions. She grew up during the Great Depression and spent all of her life afterward living frugally. From her, my grandmother learned the value of preserving her garden harvest. And I have learned to check prices twice before buying, just in case there are hidden fees or cheaper options elsewhere.

Do not be afraid to haunt sales and thrift stores. Make lists of what it is that you want or need for your practice and then browse online auctions. Save up your money and buy from small, local crafters instead of the big hobby stores. Be intentional with your spending. Remember that your economic power is a type of magic as well.

Reusing

I could write paragraphs about the concrete benefits of reusing objects. I could cite statistics about landfills and recycling. I could even tie the topic to the skill of frugality I just discussed. But I'd rather focus on the witchy reasons one would want to reuse objects. Reusing items keys into a part of our brain where creativity is stored. It asks the question, What else? What else can this be used for? What else can it do? How else can it serve?

Reusing an item honors the energy that went into making it. It's easy to look at an item—say, a jar or a small pouch—and dismiss it as something that was mass-produced and worthless once its primary purpose has passed. But that denies the object's value and ignores the work that went into it. Instead, when we look at the potential of objects beyond their original use, we're recognizing that everything can serve multiple functions, no matter the origin. As witches, we recognize that a jar isn't only a jar. It holds materia magica we've collected, it is a vessel of change where we mix our potions, it contains and intensifies our spellwork in jar spells, and it is something to drink from when we are thirsty. The uses go on and on and on. And in recognizing that a simple jar can contain multitudes, that it has more than a single purpose, we can expand that understanding to include ourselves and our world.

Reusing items in magic brings the added benefit of familiarity. When you are accustomed to a certain incense, a particular crystal, or the way your offering bowl fits into your hand, you fall into a magical mindset more easily. You cleanse your tools between uses, of course, but your relationship with them grows.

When reusing items, you need to make sure you are cleansing them. Just as you wash out jars, scrubbing out the last bits of salsa from them, you need to magically cleanse them. You don't want to use an item that is energetically crusty in your witchcraft.

Whatever path you follow should have a cleansing ritual you can use. If it doesn't, or you don't like it, a smoke cleanse with rosemary, cedar, or pine will do the job. Setting items out in the light of the noonday sun will do the same. Finally, you can use sound cleansing if you have no access to the sun or can't smoke cleanse. Ring a bell around the object while envisioning any energies attached to it being driven away by the sound. No bell? Use a sound file on your phone. The method of cleansing doesn't really matter so much as the act of it.

Being resourceful has the added benefit of expanding your resources and choices when it comes to magic. You start evaluating every item, no matter how mundane, for its possible magical uses. You start seeing the potential in every item, every situation. And by doing so, you increase your witchy knowledge and wisdom.

Suddenly, we see the variety of options open to us with regard to our spellcasting. No longer do we feel constrained or frustrated when we follow a spell and discover that we're missing an ingredient. In this scenario we make substitutions and know that the results will be the same, if not better. This is how resourcefulness leads to better spellcasting. Your confidence increases, you tailor spells to your own particular needs and resources, and you start to create your own spells rather than relying on others. You also see different ways you can get the materia magica you want for your spells. And one such way is foraging.

Foraging

Foraging is an ancient skill set that has died off in the last two centuries. Our ancestors supplemented their pantries with berries, leaves, roots, mushrooms, and bark they collected from the wilderness. Nature provided not only foodstuffs but also medicine and components for magic. Today there is a small, but growing, movement of foragers. Many on social media are teaching new generations how to identify edible plants. In this section, I'm focusing on collecting plants not for food but for magical purposes.

Since moving to Wyoming, I have spent hundreds of hours foraging. The mountains are only minutes away, and I have found a deep peace traipsing through the sagebrush and pine trees. Some days I come back with nothing; others I have a bag full of berries, sticks, rocks, and other witchy delights.

You don't have to run off to the mountains to forage, however. Local parks, empty parking lots, parkways, and backyards are all teeming with materia magica. Clover, dandelion, bindweed, goldenrod, and thistles are just some of the "weeds" you can find, in a majority of places, that have magical uses. A quick look around will turn up dozens more plants that you can use in your own practice.

If you have never foraged before, start by observing the plants around you. Take photos of those you don't recognize and identify them. Look up any magical properties they have. Pick one plant and do a deep dive into its history, magical correspondences, medicinal uses, etc. This has the added benefit of getting you acquainted with the land you are on.

The rules of foraging apply just as much to gathering plants for magic as they do to getting food:

- Don't take the first you see.
- Don't take everything you find. Leave some for others.
- Ask permission before foraging, whether that be from the owner of the land or the spirit of the plant.
- Know what it is that you are foraging before you take it.
- Take only as much as you can use.

These rules are in place to ensure the land isn't stripped of its natural resources by eager foragers. Remember, there is an entire ecosystem in play. While we witches might see clover for its protective properties, the rabbits and bees view it as a food source.

When you are foraging, you are going to the land with an attitude of openness and gratitude. You ask permission of the plant before you take anything from it. You give the plant time to respond. And if permission is granted, you thank the plant after you have taken from it. How do you know if permission has been granted? This is where your intuition and connection with the spirit of the plant come into play. I talk more about intuition in chapter 6, but I'll briefly touch on it now. When you ask for permission from the plant, it is as simple as asking, "May I please take a bit of you for my magic?" You then wait a few seconds to get feedback from the plant. This might come in the form of a feeling of peace or agreement, it might be a sweet scent released by the plant, or you might even hear a yes in your mind. On the other hand, you might feel uncomfortable, hear a negative response, or smell something sour and unpleasant, which would indicate a no. Whatever the response, you must abide by the plant's answer. If you get a yes, collect a little bit from the plant, but if it is a no, move on. This is a skill that will take time and effort to cultivate, but once you have the hang of it, you'll be able to forage quickly and easily. If you do get permission, always give thanks back to the plant. This can be in the form of verbally thanking it or pouring out a little water as an offering.

When you return home from your foraging trip, let the items you've collected rest for a few minutes outdoors if you can, to give any insects that might have been caught up the chance to make their escape. Hang up plant matter to dry. Lay out any bark, mushrooms, or woody material in a bright, sunlit spot where they can dry out. Set items that you want to charge or use as offerings on your altar. Store dried herbs and items in jars, paper bags, or cloth sacks out of direct sunlight until you are ready to use them. And always, always, always label your containers with what the contents are, when they were gathered, and perhaps also their magical uses. You don't want to end up with a collection of jars filled with brown plant matter that you can't identify.

Making Your Own Magical Tools

It isn't a huge leap from foraging to realizing you can make your own magical tools. Not to harp on this ad nauseam, but our witchy ancestors didn't go out to the nearest metaphysical shop to pick up incense, herb bundles, washes, and the like. They made their own. I've spent the last several years writing and teaching witches how to make their own tools for witchcraft. It's a skill and an activity that I believe helps us in many different ways:

- It exercises your magical knowledge.
- It gets you working with your hands, mind, and imagination.
- It gives you tools that are made to your exact requirements.
- It puts into practice your magical skills.

Making your own magical tools is an act of creation similar to magic. You start off with an intention: "I'm going to make an offering bowl." You gather your materials: in this case, air-dry clay. And then you enact the spell: making the bowl from the clay. During the process, you pour your intentions into the project until it is finished. What you are left with is something you created out of your own will that you can now use to further your witchcraft.

In making your own personal magical tools, draw upon your knowledge. If making incense, you'll absolutely want to research what herbs align with your purpose. But you can take this even further. Can you use moon water instead of regular water? Should you make your love incense on Friday to bring in Aphrodite's blessings? Take time to brainstorm all the ways you can stuff magical energies into the creative process. Journal about it. Meditate on it. Make a mind map or draw what you want to bring into the process. The point is to be mindful of what you are doing before you start.

I'm not going to go into recipes and instructions on making magical tools here. There are plenty of books that go over the specifics (I should know; I wrote two of them). But I will list some easy projects you could do further research on:

- Woodburn wooden mixing spoons with sigils or symbols to act as wands and to bring magical energies to your kitchen witchery.
- Embroider or paint a crystal grid to use on your altar.
- Create loose incense blends to burn on charcoal discs.
- Create a scrying mirror.
- Sew an altar cloth using fabric from worn-out clothes of your loved ones.
- Decoupage images of your ancestors on the outside of candleholders.
- Decorate a cinnamon stick broom with crystals and charms to serve as a ritual besom.
- Mix anointing oils to dress candles.

There are hundreds of other magical tool ideas out there that can fit your budget, expertise, and interests. Pinterest can offer up inspiration as well as tutorials. Dedicate yourself to creating one magical tool. Don't worry about it coming out Instagram perfect. Concern yourself with just making it. If you end up with something that doesn't suit your needs, well, then you'll have a greater appreciation for the artists who make magical tools professionally. But if you succeed...well, then you have unlocked a creative, magical side of yourself that had been previously unexplored. Perfect or not, you can be proud that you put in the effort.

The Magical EDC Kit

One of the keys to resourcefulness is seeing the magic in the mundane. Someday you might find yourself in a situation where you need to MacGyver a spell. If that day comes, you should be able to find what you need around you, rather than finding yourself frustrated because you don't have the exact right crystal. You can also make sure you are prepared by creating a magical EDC kit. EDC stands for "everyday carry" and refers to items that people carry with them wherever they go. The idea is popular with preppers (people who want to be prepared for the collapse of society), but it can be useful for witches as well.

My EDC kit consists of a couple of matches and a striker, a quartz crystal, and a couple packets of salt, all of which are packed into a breath mint tin. I also carry a miniature utili-tool that has a knife, scissors, and more that I can use to carve candles or forage plants. Other items I carry with me all the time that can also have magical uses are my collections of colored pens and paper. These items are all that I need to perform a quick spell, usually dealing with cleansing, if I need to.

Consider making your own EDC kit. You can use a mint tin, like I do, or a pouch. Include items that you could consider needing at one point or another. Most often, emergency spells will involve cleansing and healing. Take

Most often, emergency spells involve cleansing and healing.

that into account when you are putting together your list of what you will carry with you. Having something to represent the four elements can be a starting point. Try a stone for earth, a lighter for fire, a feather for air, and a small vial of water or perfume for water. Or carry items that are blessed on your altar, such as bandages and painkillers. Whatever you decide to carry with you, make sure it makes sense for your lifestyle and where you usually find yourself. And keep it minimal. Carrying an entire apothecary on you will just be burdensome.

~~~

We've gone through the first lesson of *A Witch Is*. If you stop here, I will consider the majority of my work done in that I have gotten you thinking differently. Once you start to see the magic in the mundane, you can't stop yourself. Everything becomes a potential magical tool. You see how, for example, air fresheners can be used in a pinch to create a charm for safe travel in your car by picking a scent that corresponds with safety, when you don't have the materials on hand to make a spell pouch from scratch. Suddenly, you are wondering about the weeds you are pulling from your garden. You find yourself looking up the magical correspondences for different symbols when deciding on a new shower curtain.

Don't let it overwhelm you. Sometimes a tea towel is just an object used to wipe up spills. But let your imagination fill in the blanks when you are planning on working a spell. Let it populate your home with items that are filled with magic. Charm your jewelry with glamour. Use color magic to choose your clothing so that it aligns with that day's goals. Spend your money mindfully and take time when picking out a new cauldron or candleholder. Be resourceful. Be witchy.
~~~

 EXERCISES 

The following exercises are designed to help you build up your resourcefulness muscles. For the exercises in this book, you can either make your notes directly in the pages of *A Witch Is*, or you can use your book of shadows (if you keep one), your journal, or a word processor file on your computer. The form of your note-taking isn't as important as you actually doing the exercises. You'll want to keep your notes, also, because later exercises in the book will come back to previous ones. Having notes on hand will allow you to check how your thoughts have evolved over the course of the book.

The Magical Kitchen Cupboard

YOU'LL NEED:

- Spices from your kitchen pantry
- Rag
- Your book of shadows (if you keep one), a few sheets of paper, or even the Notes app on your phone
- Something to write with

Most every Witchcraft 101 book will tell you about some of the magical ingredients in your pantry. Spices and herbs like cinnamon and basil are easy to point to as examples of materia magica that new witches already have in their homes. The lesson is as comforting as it is enlightening: there is magic everywhere if only you know how to look.

This exercise takes you beyond that initial lesson. Instead of giving you a list of herbs and spices that you might find in your cupboard, you are going to pull yours out and make a list of them.

And instead of having a table in this book of the magical correspondences of each spice, you are going to make your own.

Start by pulling all the spices out of your cupboard. Use the rag to dust off any bottles, jars, or pouches. Set everything out on a table where you can see it. Then in your book of shadows or on sheets of paper, write down all the spices you have. You can do this in any order you like, although listing them alphabetically might be the most helpful for the next part of this exercise.

Now comes the research portion. Go through your list and look up each spice and herb for its magical correspondences. *Cunningham's Encyclopedia of Magical Herbs* is a good resource, but don't limit yourself to one source. Look information up in other herbal books, research online, or get information from credible authorities on YouTube videos and social media. You want to have at least three different points of reference for each entry in your list. Look for overlaps in the different sources. See where they might differ and ask yourself why that might be. And check in with your gut. Does the assignment of basil to love, for example, make sense to you? Is cinnamon giving you protective vibes, or do you feel differently about it?

List out all the correspondences that are relevant to your life and magic, as well as at least one example of where you could use the spice in question magically. Keep this list near your spices so that you can consult it whenever you need to. Or you can go further and make labels to stick on your spice jars with the information. However you do it, the important thing is that you now have access to that information whenever you reach for a spice.

Seeing the Magical in the Mundane

YOU'LL NEED:

- Your book of shadows (if you keep one), a few sheets of paper, or even the Notes app on your phone
- Something to write with

In this exercise, you are going to put your thinking differently and resourcefulness skills to the test.

Take a seemingly mundane object and explore its magical properties. Write down ways you could use it in your magic and spellcasting. Start with some easy items, such as bowls and spoons, to get your creative juices flowing. Move on to items like the rags underneath your kitchen sink, the hand soap in your bathroom, the art on your walls, the knickknacks on your shelves. Write these down in a special magical correspondences table. When you are going to cast a spell, check with that table first to see if you have anything already on hand that you can use.

A Witch Is Resilient

Resilience is a word that is thrown around in various circles of late. People concerned with quality of life, mental health issues, and even productivity are all interested in the benefits of resilience. The concept has been credited with lowering stress, helping people navigate tough times, and even longevity.[4] But what does resilience have to do with witchcraft? Quite a bit, actually.

Being resilient means that you can deal with obstacles and setbacks more effectively. When our spells aren't working, or when we just aren't feeling magical, resilience helps us find our footing. There will be times when we question if the magic is even real. Or we'll be too tired to engage in even the simplest of rituals. If we cultivate resilience, we'll be better able to bounce back when the doubts start creeping in.

4. "Resilience: Build Skills to Endure Hardship," Mayo Clinic, December 23, 2023, https://www.mayoclinic.org/tests-procedures/resilience-training/in-depth/resilience/art-20046311.

This is why resilience is the second lesson in *A Witch Is*. Later on in the book, we'll talk about traits like confidence, which finds its beginning in being able to keep going even when we don't feel like it. In this chapter, we'll go over the history of witchcraft, discussing how witches have relied on their resilience for centuries to weather personal and political persecution. Then, we'll talk about how bending can serve us better than standing rigidly. Finally, we'll go over concrete steps of what to do when there are setbacks and when the magic doesn't work.

By the end of this chapter, you should have a good idea of what you can do to build resilience into your practice. While you are reading through this chapter, consider your personal circumstances and how you can apply what is written here to your day-to-day life. The two exercises at the end of the chapter will help you in this.

The Survival of Witchcraft

When we look at the history of witchcraft, we see that resilience is baked into its metaphysical DNA. Witchcraft and magic were accepted in societies around the world for the majority of ancient history. Shamans, druids, priests and priestesses, soothsayers, and healers were consulted by common folk and kings alike. With the advent of Christianity and its emphasis on one god, societal perceptions changed. Magic, outside of miracles, was considered the work of the devil, and it was church officials who determined what was a miracle and what went against the will of the Christian god.

Starting in the early fifteenth century, and lasting nearly three hundred years, religious persecution of witches picked up steam and became official. While the witch hunts had their origin in the Catholic church, governments soon got involved and many of the witch trials became more about stripping power from women who operated outside of society. The publication of the *Malleus Maleficarum*, written by Heinrich Kramer in 1486, gave "witch hunters" a blueprint for identifying and interrogating suspected witches. These witch hunters were paid by the communities they operated in to find and persecute witches. Soon, witch finding became big business.

To be clear, many of the people who were persecuted were not witches. They were men and women accused for various reasons, ranging from jealousy to a desire to take over property of the accused. Those who were practicing magic were most often working folk magic, fortune-telling, cursing, and curse removal. We can recognize that kind of magic as similar to what we work today, with its emphasis on changing circumstances to meet our own needs and desires.

In the later centuries, with the dawn of the age of reason, European governments switched the arguments against magic and witchcraft to secular rather than religious reasons. Witches were considered charlatans who scammed gullible people out of their money. Laws that outlawed witchcraft on the basis of fraud rather than affronts to the Christian god began to find their way into the books.

This scientific and secular rejection of magic continues today, although it is somewhat muddled. People will pray to saints but scoff at those who invoke other deities. They will make fun of those who read tarot cards while reading their horoscope every day. They will look down on magic practitioners while they buy lotto cards. While this is an example of hypocrisy, it also shines a light on how much people want to have magic in their lives.

While the old witch hunts have died down, oppression of witches still exists. In countries like the United States, witches face harassment and even legal action, such as the case of Beck

Lawrence, a Pagan witch who has been threatened with arrest because "fortune-telling" is illegal in the state of Pennsylvania, where they read tarot for clients.[5] In some countries in Africa, women and children are being targeted for abuse, mutilation, and even death, over accusations of witchcraft.[6]

From witch hunts to modern-day oppression of witches around the world, witches and witchcraft have persevered. Despite government and religious attempts to suppress it, witchcraft has gained a nominal measure of acceptance in various parts of the world and has grown over the last few decades. This grit and determination can be useful on an individual level as you practice your craft.

When There Are Setbacks

We've all been there: you had a ritual planned out and then something popped up to keep you from doing it, or you got your spell components together only to discover that the crystal you were going to use had gone missing, or your pet knocked over your altar, destroying all your spellwork. These and other setbacks can range from merely irritating to making you want to forget magic all together. What do you do when you run into an obstacle and feel like giving up?

There will always be setbacks when it comes to magic. You can adopt a resilient mindset to overcome them, however. Tools such

5. Erica Russell and Ryan Reichard, "Pennsylvania Police 'Threaten to Arrest' Metaphysical Shop Owner for Reading Tarot Cards," Loudwire, last modified December 16, 2023, https://loudwire.com/pennsylvania-police-threaten-arrest-metaphysical-shop-owner-reading-tarot-cards/.

6. Joan Nyanyuki, "Witch-Hunts and Ritual Abuse Are a Stain on Africa. We Must Confront Them," *The Guardian*, June 8, 2022, https://www.theguardian.com/global-development/commentisfree/2022/jun/08/witch-hunts-ritual-child-abuse-albinism-africa.

as visualization, outside support, and resourcefulness will help you to face those challenges.

Visualization

One aspect of witchcraft that will get brought up again and again in *A Witch Is* is visualization, the key to magic. Visualization will give you the means to overcome a great majority of your obstacles. If, for example, it is raining on the night of the full moon when you are going to perform an outdoor ritual, move indoors. The moon is still there. You only have to use your own visualization skills to fill in the gaps.

Your visualization powers are necessary when performing magic to overcome your obstacles as well. You need to be able to see the results you want as if they have already happened for the magic to work. This is where activities like meditation and journaling can prove helpful. You can imagine all the ways your spell could work and home in on the one that you want. Then, when you have built the result you want, you can use it in your spellcasting.

Despite the name, visualization doesn't have to be limited to the sense of sight. Visualization is creating a sensory experience as clearly as possible. So if you are visually impaired or find it difficult to create a vision in your mind, make use of your other senses. Smell, touch, hearing, and taste can all be used in visualization. Instead of seeing an apple, taste or smell it. Or when visualizing the outcome of your spellwork, imagine how it will feel, what it will sound like, and what emotions success will bring with it.

Support System

No man is an island. The same goes for witches. Having a support system is helpful when faced with setbacks. This support system gives you not only people you can turn to in times of trouble, but also people you can bounce ideas off of, people you can brainstorm with, and even people to perform rituals and magic with. These don't have to be other witches, although that might be helpful in some cases. For me, one member of my support team is my therapist, who is a Pagan and understands much of what I mean when I talk about my practice. Family and friends, even if they don't fully understand, as long as they are supportive, can offer you encouragement.

There are also many online communities of witches that you can tap into for support and guidance. There is a plethora of narrowly focused groups, such as ones for Appalachia witches or ones that cover only kitchen witchery. With all that variety, you are sure to find one that fits your witchcraft style. Be discerning when joining a community. Take time to get to know it, learn its rules and customs, and evaluate the interactions of the members before you dive in. If a group should prove not to be what you are looking for, move on to another. It might take time to find one where you feel comfortable, and that is okay. You are looking for a community where you can get and give support, so you are allowed to take your time in your search.

Once you have one or more individuals in your support team, you want to check in with them regularly, even when things are going well. You also want to be there for those others. This is a reciprocal relationship after all, and it will only grow stronger the more each party leans on the other. Be willing to provide support, lend an ear to listen to frustrations and questions, offer a shoulder to cry on, or be there in whatever way you would want them to be there for you.

Get Resourceful

Much like with visualization, being resourceful will help you when you hit setbacks such as not having the right materia magica on hand or finding that you can't perform a spell exactly the way you had planned. Take, for example, magical timing. The classical planets are associated not only with particular days of the week but with hours of those days. If you want to cast your self-confidence spell now, instead of waiting for Tuesday, you can find the hours that are related to Mars and cast it then. I go more into the planetary hours in the "Magical Timing for Better Spellcasting" section on page 82.

For myself, I created a spell to aid in writing this book. I wanted to work with Neptune and its influence over creative inspiration. Neptune isn't associated with days of the week or even hours. But with research, I learned that Neptune is a higher vibration of Venus, and therefore, I could use Venus's timing associations for my spellcasting. I could have also dropped Neptune entirely and gone with timing associated with Mercury and its emphasis on communication, if I had wanted. By taking time to look into all my options and being flexible in my thinking, I came up with a solution.

You can do the same as long as you take a step back when faced with obstacles. If you don't have on hand the items your spell calls for, use substitutions. If you can't use incense to smoke cleanse your space for whatever reason, use a different cleansing technique, such as sound. Don't get so caught up in how magic "should" be done that you don't even attempt the spell because everything isn't perfect. Remember, magic is ultimately fueled by you, not the various tools, materia magica, and props that we think we need.

When the Magic Isn't Working

You can schedule time for your rituals. You can check in with your community when you hit obstacles. You can substitute an exotic materia magica for one that you have in your apothecary. And yet there will come a time when it feels like nothing you do is working. Your candle refuses to burn all the way down, or the incense won't light. The freezer spell you worked on the obnoxious coworker seems to have backfired because now you have been assigned to work with them on a project. Maybe you just don't see results despite having done everything you can think of to set your spell up for success. There are things you can do to bounce back from these annoyances. You can reevaluate your goals, take a step back, and do some digging through divination.

Change Your Goals

We turn to three actions you can take when the magic doesn't work: evaluate your situation, see if your actions are suited to the situation, and change tactics if necessary. In this case, if you aren't seeing results with your spellcasting, it might be because you are trying to do too much, or you might be focusing on the wrong outcomes. This is often the case when witches first start out and jump right into casting spells without laying the groundwork for success. They want to make big changes, but they aren't prepared.

So if your magic isn't working, check to see that you have clear goals. Yes, you might be casting a spell to bring love into your life, but are you clear on what kind of partner you are looking for? Or perhaps you are looking to bring in more money. Have you established how that is going to happen, or are you just throwing a handful of mint at the universe and hoping for the best? This is where you need to have clear goals.

It might seem pedestrian, but writing down what it is that you want your spell to accomplish can go a long way to getting in the right mindset for successful magic. Consider what your goal is and then see if you can break it down into smaller, more manageable chunks. Take the money example from the previous paragraph: maybe instead of just inviting the universe to send you more money (which can result in finding some loose change in your couch), you look at how you want that money to come to you. If you have a side hustle, perhaps you focus instead on finding more clients. If you have a regular job, perhaps you focus on smoothing the way for a promotion.

We'll dive more in depth into how to set specific goals on page 152. For the moment, however, keep in mind that goals that are well defined are going to have more success than those that are nebulous.

Support Your Magic

Related to setting specific goals is the notion that you need to do the mundane work for your spell to see results. Magic on its own is less effective than when it is supported by other actions. You can light rosemary incense and set fluorite crystals on your desk to help you pass a test, but if you don't also study, the magic will fizzle out.

This again goes back to doing the work before you actually cast your spell. Devote as much time to thinking of what you can do mundanely to accomplish your goals as you do to choosing what materia magica you will include in your spell. Doing so might give you ideas of other ways you can include magic in your efforts. For example, if you are going into an interview, you might cast a spell ahead of time to make your interviewer view you more favorably. As you are preparing for that spell, you think about ways you can help that magic along, from deciding what you will wear to brainstorming responses to possible interview questions. And as you do this work, you realize you can work color magic into your wardrobe and add invisible sigils to the résumé you bring with you. Now you are weaving magic into your actions, rather than simply casting a spell.

Refresh Your Spirit

Another way you can overcome your magic not working is to take a step back. We can get into a habit of casting spell after spell after spell when we don't see results. I've been a victim of the mindset that if at first it didn't succeed, I should try again. That kind of thinking leads to burnout and backlash as the universe sees us banging our heads against the metaphysical wall. If you keep casting spells and not seeing anything happen, it might be time to take a break.

This is where taking a walk in nature, meditating, or even just grounding yourself can help. You might also engage in other activities that are completely separate from witchcraft to give your mind a bit of a break. Activities like creating a mandala, baking, engaging in a craft, putting together a puzzle, or reading can distract the conscious part of your mind, allowing the subconscious mind to work through the problem of your magic not working.

Taking a step back also helps take the pressure off.

Taking a step back also helps take the pressure off you to perform. Yes, we want to live magical lives filled with potions, dried herb bundles, beautifully curated altars, and one of those floppy witch hats that are seemingly everywhere these days, but even magical creatures need a break. Engage in some self-care and recognize that sometimes you need to give your witchy self a rest. Once you have taken some time to recuperate, you can return to your practice, renewed.

Check In with the Universe

Finally, if you keep throwing spells out into the universe but aren't seeing any results, it's time to do some research. You can check in with your support team, but you can also turn to divination. It's always a good idea to get an outside perspective when things go awry. Factors can change, and what might have been a good idea the day before may be a dud now.

You should have a divination form that you are comfortable with. Tarot is one of the most popular forms of divination, but there are plenty of others, including runes, scrying, pendulums, and more, that can be used to find out why your magic isn't working. Ask your divination method questions like these: What is keeping my spell from working? What can I do to see the results I want from this spell? What obstacles are getting in the way of my spellwork?

Give the answers you receive all due consideration. We all have blind spots, and yours might be interfering with your spellcasting. Maybe you are lacking self-confidence in your ability to work magic. Or perhaps you are tackling the wrong problem, and there's a better way to get what you want. It could be that there are outside forces working against you. Whatever it is, you won't know until you dig deep. Once you have an answer, you are halfway to figuring out a solution.

~~~~
~~~~

No matter what your path or practice, resilience is one of the most powerful tools you can have in your toolbox when it comes to magic. A witch must be ready to persevere in the face of prejudice, despite hardship, and when things go wrong. This skill will help keep you going when you feel like giving up. It gives you extra strength that you can draw on when you might feel that you are out of reserves. And it ties you to the generations of witches who came before you and those who will come after.

 EXERCISES 

Resilience is a trait you can build. Doing so gives your magic greater flexibility to overcome obstacles. The following exercises are designed to help you practice resilience in your everyday life.

Fortify Yourself

YOU'LL NEED:

- Your book of shadows (if you keep one), a few sheets of paper, or even the Notes app on your phone
- Something to write with

Much of resilience comes from preparation. If you can spend a few minutes thinking about how you would handle certain situations, then you aren't caught flat-footed when the unexpected happens. To that end, this exercise is meant to help you come up with ways that you will fortify yourself when the worst happens. You will write this list down somewhere you can refer to it when needed. This can mean writing it in your book of shadows (if you have one), in your planner or journal, or even as a note in your phone. The point is to have the list somewhere accessible to you.

Your list can involve things like magical baths, meditations, listening to uplifting music, going for a run, grounding yourself, or anything else that makes you feel good about yourself. This is self-care with the goal of helping you weather any self-doubt. Once you have made your list, you want to then make sure you have what you need on hand for your activities. If you find that a long soak helps you clear your mind and feel better, make sure you have bath salts, candles, oils, or whatever else you like to add to your baths in stock. Make a playlist of music that gets your blood pumping. Have shoes and socks near the door for when you need to take a walk.

The point of this exercise is to make it as easy as possible for you to fortify yourself when you need to. When you suffer setbacks or face obstacles, you will be more likely to take the time to engage in self-care if you have already put in the effort previously. Consider it a gift from present you to future you.

Everyday Magic

You'll need:

- Your book of shadows (if you keep one), a few sheets of paper, or even the Notes app on your phone
- Something to write with

Just as you looked at mundane objects in the "Seeing the Magical in the Mundane" exercise on page 25, you will be doing something similar here. You are going to make a list of the activities you engage in on a daily basis and then find ways that you can make them magical. By doing so, you build resilience into your daily schedule so that when you feel like you haven't done anything witchy in a while, you can look at your life and see that you are still practicing your magic. This also sets you up to better overcome obstacles when they crop up, as you can find magical solutions to them because you are already thinking magically daily.

To make a list of daily activities, start with imagining a typical day in your life. From the time you wake up until the time you go to bed, list out your standard routine. Do you shower in the morning? Eat breakfast first and then get dressed for the day? Do you get a lunch break at work? What is the first thing you do when you get home? What is your evening routine like? Cover everything you do regularly.

Once you have a list, it's time to look at how you could add magic to each activity. Can you include color or scent magic in your makeup routine? Can you add affirmations to your toothbrushing? Look at your jewelry; can you turn it into a confidence-boosting charm? Can you add a spell pouch or crystals to just inside your door to cleanse and protect you when you enter and leave your home? Think about all the ways you practice magic and how you can work it into your daily life to elevate the mundane to magical.

While you are going to consider all the activities in your daily schedule, you are only going to pick one or two to make magical. Pick the ones that most appeal to you and seem like they would be the easiest to ritualize in your day-to-day routine. Now start doing them. If you choose to record your dreams, for example, make sure you have a dream journal next to your bed. Add a sachet of mugwort, lavender, and morning glory seeds under your pillow to help you remember your dreams. Set your alarm five minutes earlier so you have time to write in your journal. Do what you have to to set yourself up for success.

A Witch Is Creative

In my work as a sewist and then a writer, I have had a lot of time to think about creativity. Our society has a love-hate relationship with artistic expression. We line up to see movies, listen to musical artists, or hang art on our walls, but then we devalue the work that goes into those projects by paying artists pennies for their efforts. The rise of generative AI, in which the human factor is taken out of the artistic process, is just the latest iteration of this attitude.

The byproduct of society's treatment of the arts and artists is the belief held by a large part of the population that they are not creative. I have heard some version of "Oh, I'm not creative" more times than I can count. We have elevated creativity to some rarified talent that only a few have. Arts and artists are fenced off from the general population as something special. The truth is that humans as a whole are creative. Our ability to turn our imagination into reality is fundamental to the human experience. It has only been society's insistence that art and creation can only happen under specific conditions and by certain people that has kept us from recognizing our own creative talents.

What, you might be asking, does this have to do with witchcraft? The answer is: everything.

Magic as an Act of Creation

Aleister Crowley defined magic as "the Science and Art of causing Change to occur in conformity with Will."[7] While the quote focuses on the action of making change, there is a process that happens before the act: imagining the change you want to enact.

There are multiple parts to magic. You must first decide what it is you want to do. Then you visualize the process and outcome. You choose the spell components you'll need, the timing, the words. Only then, after all that pre-spell work, do you engage in the spell. Those steps you take before the actual work all involve your creative faculties. If you do not lay down the groundwork before you cast your spell, it won't be as effective.

This is why I say that magic is an act of creation. Every step of the way, you are engaging your creativity: from imagining your desired outcome to choosing your materia magica to performing the spell. You are participating in the same creative act that is found in nature. Magic creates a new and different reality, of which we are the architects.

Creating Your Own Spells and Rituals

When we start our witchcraft practice, it can be overwhelming. There are so many questions that plague us. Do we have the right materials? Are we saying the right words? Will our magic work, or is it just a bunch of hocus pocus? We are fortunate to live in a

7. Aleister Crowley, *Magick in Theory and Practice* (Lecram Press, 1929), xvi.

time when there is a plethora of resources for new witches. Books and social media have all sorts of information and advice on how to cast magic. With just a little research, you can find instructions for whatever spell you need, usually accompanied by aesthetically pleasing photos and enchanting music.

I'm not disparaging these resources. I still avail myself of them. But there comes a time when you will find you need to go beyond Pinterest spells. You may not be able to find exactly what you need. Or you might not have the spell components on hand that the spell calls for. Or it might instruct you to do something you aren't comfortable with doing. After all, not all spellwork is comfortable for all witches. For example, I hate speaking aloud when I am working on my spells. I also have no talent for writing chants or rhymes. Because of this, I don't incorporate chants in my spellcasting. Finally, you might just want to create your own spells. That's when you tap into your creativity.

Creating your own spells and rituals needn't be intimidating.

Creating your own spells and rituals needn't be intimidating. There are several ways to do so, but first you need to decide what kind of spellwork and magic best fits your personality and tastes. We'll cover figuring out what magic best works for you in the "Finding Your Personal Path" section on page 118. All you need to know now, however, is that working with magic that aligns with your tastes and style gives you a framework for creating your own spells. If, for example, you are more attuned to crystals, you'll want to include them in your spellwork, perhaps in a crystal grid or in enchanted jewelry.

To create your own spells, you want to first identify the problem you want to solve with magic. This seems like an obvious step, but too often we don't spend enough time really thinking about the problem, and thus, our solutions don't actually address the real issue. You may know that you want to feel better about yourself, but if you don't do a little soul-searching, you might think you just need to work a self-love spell when what is really bothering you is unacknowledged childhood trauma. You will be treating the symptoms rather than the cause of the problem. This and the next step are where you should focus the bulk of your energy. If you do so, your magic is much more likely to work.

Once you've identified the problem, you want to decide on your desired solution or outcome. This is where your creativity really comes into play through visualization. You need to be able to picture, in detail, what your life would be like if this problem were no longer an issue. The more detailed your answer to this question, the more likely you are to get what you want from your magic. Taking the above example into consideration, if you have determined that the problem with your self-confidence is that you were belittled as a child, you want to focus on how that manifests currently and what your life would look like if it no longer bothered you. How would you carry yourself? What would it feel like to be free of those memories of your childhood trauma? What sort of life would you lead if you weren't always plagued with the words that hurt you? Be specific. Really get into your visualization to picture how much better off you would be without that old trauma weighing you down.

Now that you have a picture of what your outcome is, it's time to decide on the best kind of magic to address the problem and bring about the solution. This is where your preferred method of magic comes into play. Maybe you are drawn to green magic and wish to make a tincture to help lessen the impact of those trauma-filled memories. Perhaps you need to engage in shadow work. Or maybe you use the elements to create a ritual of letting go. However you best experience magic, you want to incorporate those elements into your spellwork or ritual. If you are at a loss for what kind of magic would best suit your problem, use divination as an aid. We'll go over how to divine before working a spell in chapter 9. All you need to know now is that divination is a great tool to use before you cast your spell. And don't neglect to check in with your intuition. Oftentimes, that will lead you to the right magic.

Once you have decided on the type of spell you are going to cast, it's time to find out what you need for the spell. This is when you will decide on timing, spell components, and even what you will wear and where you will perform the spell. There are plenty of guidebooks that provide information on correspondences, magical timing, and so on. My advice is to find at least three different resources that you can cross-check when deciding on spell components. Use those things that make sense to you and that you have access to. Remember your lessons on resourcefulness from chapter 1.

Be as specific as possible with this step. If you are going to speak words or a chant, nail down the wording. Memorize it so that you won't be stumbling over the words when you are engaged in the spell. Use your visualization once again to see how the spell will look when you perform it. Figure out where you will get the things you will need for the spell. Decide if you will be casting a circle or sacred space before you cast your spell and how you will release the magic once you are done. Make sure the clothing you are going to be wearing is clean and ready. Mark off the time for your spell or ritual on your calendar.

Do not neglect the mundane aspect of your spellcasting at this point. You need to decide what you will do physically to support it. Going back to our self-confidence issue, think about what you can do that doesn't involve witchcraft. Will you be going to therapy? Getting medication to deal with the anxiety that is entwined with those issues? Will you be going no contact with those people who undermined your self-esteem? Does the way forward call for forgiveness? Magic works in tandem with concrete, mundane actions. You need both to overcome the problems that you face.

At this point, it is a good idea to write down or otherwise record your spell steps and instructions. If you keep a book of shadows or a journal, that is where you would write down everything to do with your spell. Don't feel like you have to use words: you can draw the steps, create a mind map, or even make a collage. If you aren't a visual or wordy person, you could try using a voice recorder to document your spell. The benefit of recording the spell before you perform it is threefold. First, it gets you comfortable with the steps before you actually cast the spell. This keeps you from stumbling, having to look things up, or otherwise halting your momentum once you get started. Second, it gives you a place to then come back to and record what the outcome of your spell is. Doing so will boost your self-confidence when it comes to spellcasting, but it also gives you a place to troubleshoot if the spell didn't work the way you wanted it to. Finally, by recording your spell, you start your own record of spells that you can come back to when you are facing a similar situation in the future. You've already done the legwork that your future self can benefit from.

After you have gone through all the above steps, it is time to collect your spell components, get your space ready, and cast your spell or perform your ritual. If you have done all the prep work ahead of time, you should be able to cast the magic from memory without having to pause to see what to do next. The steps will come naturally as you flow from one to the next. And that ease will inform your magic, giving it a better chance of working. Once the spell is cast, you get started on the mundane work you've identified to support your magic.

Creating your own spells and rituals gives you flexibility in your magical practice. It allows you to create solutions that are suited for your own unique situation. And it helps you exercise your creative muscles. All of this is made possible by the most important tool in the witch's toolbox: visualization. And we'll cover that next.

Visualization: The Witch's Secret Sauce

Without visualization, there is no magic. How can we enact change if we cannot imagine it? Likewise, many aspects of magic, such as energies and spirits, do not operate on a level that can be perceived by our physical senses, not without the help of visualization. In order to direct our magic, then, we must have a way to experience it, and this is where visualization comes into play.

When it comes to visualization, two factors can get in the way of successful spellcasting. One is that visualization doesn't come easily to everyone. The second is the emphasis on the visual aspect of the action. Either one can derail a witch whether they are new to the craft or a seasoned professional.

Let's start with the fact that visualization is a tool that requires practice. Think of it as a muscle. If you were starting an exercise program, you wouldn't immediately grab the one-hundred-pound dumbbells. You would start with smaller weights, training your way up. The same can be said with visualization. Many books, blog posts, and videos tell you to visualize this or that without going into how to actually do it. There is an expectation that people will just know that visualization is akin to imagination and leave it at that. Visualization is simply using our imagination to perceive that which is otherwise undetectable.

The problem arises if you are a person who hasn't indulged in your imagination. It might feel silly to do so, or you might not know where to begin. If you feel awkward with visualization, try this exercise: Rub your palms together for thirty seconds and then hold them an inch or two apart. You will feel a sensation between your palms. Perhaps it will be a tingling or a feeling of pressure. It could even be a crackling as if the space between your hands is charged.

Now, as you feel this sensation, imagine what that energy between your palms looks like. What color is it? What shape? This exercise works because you can feel the energy but can't see it, thus forcing your imagination to fill in the blanks.

Because visualization is like a muscle, you need to practice it regularly to keep it in tip-top shape. If you are constantly casting spells, engaged in ritual, or addressing spirits and deities, you will be using your visualization often. If not, you can engage in guided meditations, scrying, or daydreaming to strengthen that muscle. Ideally, you are practicing visualization every day.

What if you are practicing daily and you still can't visualize anything? In that case, it might be that you are focusing on the wrong sense. While many people are visually inclined, there are just as many whose strongest sense isn't sight-based. Perform the hand exercise from above, but this time focus on other senses. What does the sensation smell or sound like? Does it instead have a taste? It might, perhaps, simply exist as a sensation. If one of your other senses dominates, you might be better off utilizing it in your visualization. So, for example, instead of "seeing" negative energy as black smoke, you might instead smell something rotten. Then, instead of visualizing the smoke being blown away, you smell a sweet scent replacing the rotten one as the negative energy is cleansed from your space.

However you visualize it is valid. Magic and witchcraft are personal, so it makes sense that the action underpinning them would also reflect the personality of individual witches.

Visualization taps into your creative side. Not only does it help you keep your outcome in mind, but it allows you to experience the imperceptible parts of magic. Spend time finding the type of visualization that works for you and then practice it. The more you practice, the stronger your visualization will be. Eventually, you might even be able to cast magic with nothing but your intent and visualization.

The Astral Residence

When it comes down to it, you don't actually need all the materia magica, tools, and other occult objects to cast magic. Intention and visualization are all you need to enact your will through witchcraft. The other items all can help focus your intention and aid in visualization, however, and they can help set the mood, which can increase your self-confidence as you cast your spells. But what if I told you that you could have access to all the mood-setting, aesthetically pleasing magical accoutrements, all without spending a dime or even leaving your home? What I'm talking about is creating an astral residence in which to cast your magic with nothing more than the power of your mind.

The astral residence is a concept I first encountered in Edain McCoy's *A Witch's Guide to Faery Folk.*[8] In McCoy's book, the astral

8. Edain McCoy, *A Witch's Guide to Faery Folk: How to Work with the Elemental World* (Llewellyn, 2002), 119–21.

residence is a space a witch creates in their mind from which they can astral project, meditate, and even work magic, notably in conjunction with working with faery folk.

This is a bit of advanced magic, and you'll want to have a strong ability to visualize to create your astral temple. However, once you have established it, you will find that there are no limits to the kinds of spells you can cast or magic you can work. Whatever you need, you can bring to mind for use. You can even work with timing, moving your astral residence forward or backward in time to take advantage of specific astronomical events.

I love this concept, as it allows one to work great magic without any physical tools. All you need is your visualization. However, building an astral residence may be difficult for those who have conditions such as aphantasia, an inability to visualize. In those cases, you may be able to still build your astral residence by stating to yourself what you are doing or using senses other than imagery to create it.

Building Your Astral Residence

To begin, you want to decide how your astral residence will look and feel. My own is a log cabin in the middle of the woods. You might want a cottage, a luxury high rise, a temple, or merely a clearing in a forest. Spend a good amount of time on this step. Write out the description in your journal or sketch it out. You can even make a collage on paper or digitally.[9] Your astral residence may evolve and change once you've been using it for a while, but you need a starting point.

Once you have created your blueprint for it, take time to visualize being in it. This is just a practice run before you actually enter

9. Pinterest or apps like Canva are especially useful for this.

the astral residence. Imagine what it is like to be in that space. What does it feel like? Sound like? Smell like? Imagine touching the furniture, looking out the windows. What do your footsteps sound like when you walk? Feel what the air temperature is like. You are trying to build as clear and detailed a picture of your astral residence as possible at this point.

When you are satisfied that you have created as complete an image as you can, it's time to visit your astral residence. This is a process that will require quiet and uninterrupted time. Make sure that your phone is turned to silent. Get rid of any distractions so that you can give all your concentration to this first visit.

Start by lying or sitting down comfortably. Close your eyes and relax your breathing. You want to go inside your mind, and one of the easiest ways is the stairway method. Visualize ten steps descending in front of you. At the bottom is a closed door. Descend the steps, counting down from ten as you do so, stepping down with each number. See the door getting closer as you go down the steps. Once you have reached the number one, you should be standing in front of the door. Reach out, open it, and step through into your astral residence.

Inside it should match what you already imagined, although there might be slight changes as your mind adjusts the blueprint to something better suited to your needs. Take time to explore the area. Make note of any changes. Add anything that you now realize is missing. Take a seat and just soak up the atmosphere of this magical place you've created.

After a few minutes, it is time to leave your astral residence. Exit via the door you came in by. Walk up the stairs, counting from one to ten as you do so. When you reach ten, open your eyes and wriggle your toes and fingers to anchor yourself back into your physical body.

Using Your Astral Residence

Now that you have established your astral residence, it is time to use it. The more you do so, the easier it will be. To start with, you'll need to lay down a magical protection over the space. While the astral residence is in your mind, you still want to protect it against any malicious magic, any negative energies or spirits that might be attracted to your work in it, and self-doubt and self-sabotage.

Start by returning to your astral residence using the stairway method. Once inside, decide how you are going to protect your space. You can lay down a crystal grid, create a witch ball, plant protective herbs and plants around the space, and so on. Just keep in mind that whatever type of protection magic you choose, you will have to regularly refresh it to keep it potent. My preferred method is a shield spell. I have marked the boundaries of my astral residence by placing a bubble of protection around it. When it is time to refresh that protective shield, I stand at the edge of my boundary and envision a bubble of white light surrounding the entirety of the astral residence. The bubble reaches up into the sky and down into the ground, to contain the space. I charge the bubble with the task of keeping out anything that I don't specifically allow into the space. I have been casting this bit of magic so long that I am able to tell when it needs to be refreshed by feeling alone. Until you can do that, you should refresh your protections on a regular basis, perhaps doing so every third time you visit your astral residence or during the full moon or the solstices. The point is to pick a schedule and stick with it.

While the astral residence is in your mind, you still want to protect it.

Casting spells in your astral residence works the same as it would in the physical realm. You start with intention and use your visualization to fuel the spell.

The benefit of working said magic in your astral residence is that whatever tools, materia magica, or other spell components you want to include in your spellwork are immediately available. There is no exotic herb or expensive gemstone that is out of your reach. If you have always wanted a large copper cauldron for making potions but live in a small apartment, you can now have it. You can have the stocked apothecary of your dreams. The silver athame, the crystal ball, even the ritual wear—it is all just a matter of your visualization. And while you don't need any of that to cast magic, I won't deny that there is something very satisfying about being able to make all your witchy dreams come true when practicing your craft.

Start small, with spells that you have cast before, or with magic that you are confident in working. Spells that target your mental, physical, and emotional health are often more effective coming from the astral residence. Visit your space regularly to get comfortable working in it and to keep your visualization sharp. Don't be afraid to play around with your space and with your imagination. Change things up or around to suit your current magical needs. The astral residence shouldn't be a stagnant place.

On Familiars, Spirits, and Deities

Your astral residence doesn't have to be a place that only you visit. In my own, my pets who have passed away have all taken up residence in the space. They don't act as familiars but instead provide a comforting presence when I need it. You can, however, envision a familiar in yours. This can be one that you already have in your physical life, or it can be one that you have created to aid you in your magic. Whichever it is, you will have to treat it as you would a physical animal. This means treating it with kindness and respect and ensuring that your astral residence has the requisite materials for its needs. Make sure you interact with your familiar regularly, to forge and maintain the bond needed for it to help you with your magic.

Other spirits and even deities can be invited into your astral residence as well. These are not entities of your imagination but actual individuals and should be treated as such. But if you decide to open your space to them, they can be a source of great aid and information. I have worked with Hestia and Hekate in the past in my astral residence. I also have other spirits, such as a water hag that lives in a well on the land and provides me with magical water for my spellwork. Your magical protections will keep spirits and even deities from entering your space if you don't want them to. If your protections have weakened and you come to your astral residence to find spirits there, you can ask them politely to leave. If they refuse, a liberal application of salt, iron, or blackthorn will send them packing. Make sure to refresh your protective barriers after the spirits leave.

Keep in mind that, like with magic cast in the physical world, the magic you work in your astral residence will require you to follow up with concrete, mundane actions. Use your astral residence not only as a place to practice your magic but also as a place to meditate, rest, and reconnect with your inner self and even as a place for study. As it is a place in your mind, it will always be a safe space from which you can expand your magical practice.

~~~

Being a witch is an act of creation, and as you are a witch, you must therefore possess creativity. By creating your own spells and rituals, you are engaging with witchcraft just as our magical ancestors did. Continue to cultivate your visualization and visit your astral residence often, and you'll find yourself becoming more and
~~~

more comfortable with practicing witchcraft without the input of books and spells written by others.

 EXERCISES 

The two exercises for this chapter are meant to get you tapping into your creativity with regard to your magic. Take your time with each one and exercise those creative, magical muscles.

Creating Your Own Magical Correspondences

YOU'LL NEED:

- Your book of shadows (if you keep one), a few sheets of paper, or even the Notes app on your phone
- Something to write with

While there are plenty of books and websites out there that will list the correspondences for various herbs, crystals, symbols, and the like, it behooves the witch to find correspondences that work for their individual needs. Sometimes this is just a matter of comparing various sources to drill down on the specific materia magica you need. But there are times when those lists will leave you cold, giving correspondences that just don't work for you.

This is when the witch takes a walk down their own correspondences path. It is time to figure out your own magical correspondences for the materia magica that you will use in your practice. This exercise is especially useful for figuring out the magical properties of items that don't usually find their way onto such lists. This includes symbols and everyday items and materials.

Start with the list of symbols and objects below. Write what first comes to mind when you think of them. This is your intuition talking to you about what your personal correspondences are. Write down what emotions, deities, natural phenomena, colors, directions, and more that come to mind. At this point, you are just brainstorming, so don't revise as you go—just let the thoughts flow.

- Apple
- Heart
- Thread
- Knot
- Feather
- Sparrow
- Mouse
- Spoon
- Bed
- Shoes

Once you have gotten your intuitive thoughts on paper, you can go through the list and consider each symbol and how the correspondences you came up with fit or don't fit. This is when you can turn to things like meditation or even divination to go deeper into the meanings you came up with. You want to stick with correspondences that make sense to you. Check in with your body. Does the meaning feel good when you associate it with that particular symbol? Or do you feel tension when you equate the two?

This practice gets you to start thinking outside the established correspondences and get more personal in your magic. Look around yourself and pick two or three objects that you can see. Go through the same exercise as you did with the list above. When you have a dream, write down the symbols from it and figure out your personal correspondences for them. When you are out in the world, do the same. As you get more comfortable with creating your own correspondences, you will find that there are so many more ways to cast spells and practice magic without "traditional" magic tools. Being aware of what you personally consider magical will also help you be aware of signs from the universe as you go about your day-to-day life.

Back to the Magical Pantry

You'll need:

- Your list from "The Magical Kitchen Cupboard" exercise on page 23
- Something to write with

Take the list of herbs and their correspondences you wrote and sit down with them. Look over the list and start coming up with substitutions that you could use instead of the items you already have on hand. Don't focus solely on herbal substitutions. Crystals, colors, and objects can all be used as substitutes in your magical practice. You can reference the list of symbols and objects that you have already created magical correspondences for in the exercise above.

The point of the exercise is to get you comfortable with using your creativity when you cast magic, especially magic you get from books and websites. This ties into the lessons on resourcefulness, but this time you are tapping into your own innate wisdom, rather than taking information from other sources. Magic is personal, and as such, those materia magica and tools that you have a connection with through your personal correspondences will achieve better results.

Once you have come up with your substitutions, keep the list with your original list. Add to it when you think of new substitutions. Consult it whenever you are creating a spell to see what your options are for tools and components. You will come back to this list again later in the book, so keep it in a safe place.

A Witch Is Kind

If the last three chapters dealt with the mental aspects of witchcraft, this one deals with the heart of it. Kindness gets a bad rap these days due to the way American society treats it. Our society has, over the years, framed kindness as weakness. And in an environment of toxic masculinity, "I got mine, screw you" mentalities, and just general meanness of spirit, the last thing people want to be viewed as is weak. Being weak, we are told, opens us up to bullying, to being taken advantage of, and to becoming victims.

However, kindness is a strength to be fostered. I'd go so far as to say that witches can't help but be kind because they see the vulnerability and interconnectedness of everyone and everything. Being kind does not mean that witches cannot work in their own interests or in their own defense. It does not even rule out offensive magic and flat-out vengeance. Whereas niceness can lead to problematic behavior like spiritual bypassing[10] and victim blaming, kindness keeps us open and accountable to ourselves.

But what is kindness? It is a state of being that is characterized by warmth, acting on the behalf of others without an expectation of getting anything in return, and being concerned with people, entities, and the world at large around you. It is a way of thinking and acting that doesn't center solely on yourself but takes into account your position in relation to others and the world. It does not mean that you are elevating others over yourself, because you need to have kindness for your own person as well. It simply means that you are aware that everything is interconnected and actions you take can have an effect on others. And because of all this, the witch who is kind knows to make sure they are aware of the possible outcomes and consequences of casting spells and other actions.

So if you have a negative reaction to the idea that to be a witch is to be kind, it's time to do some deep work into why that is. Perhaps, like me, you dealt with a lot of childhood trauma or abuse at the hands of people you trusted. Maybe you see the world, in the state it is today, and can't see a reason for kindness. Whatever the reason, take the time to figure out why the concept of kindness bothers you. Divination can help with this. Ask questions like "What is the underlying reason I am reacting this way to the idea of kindness?" and "What is blocking me from seeing kindness as a strength?" You can even go so far as to ask, "What am I missing in my life due to not expressing kindness?" and "What do I gain from expressing kindness?"

10. Spiritual bypassing means using spiritual concepts to avoid, or "bypass," facing complex emotions and psychological issues. The concept was introduced by John Welwood in the 1980s.

You can also engage in shadow work to answer those questions by journaling. Write with the following prompts in mind:

- When was a time I experienced kindness? How did it make me feel?
- When was a time I was kind to someone? What was their reaction?
- What emotions come up when I think about kindness?
- What do I think would be the outcome if I were a kinder person?

Even if you are not convinced at this point that kindness is necessary for witchcraft, these exercises are helpful in being more self-aware.

Why is kindness important to the witch? It keeps us cognizant of the interconnectedness of the world. In knowing that we are all entangled with everything else—our neighbors, our yards, our planet, even—we take care when we cast our magic. We don't send spells out willy-nilly without taking a moment to consider the consequences. Kindness also provides a framework for the ethics of witchcraft. It tells us that we have the right to defend ourselves, to teach others lessons, and to enrich ourselves, as long as we are measured and thoughtful in our spellcasting.

Kind Does Not Equal Nice

One of my husband's favorite movies is *Road House*. One line from it tends to sum up his philosophy: "Be nice until it's time to not be nice."[11] The concept sounds simple enough: give the benefit

11. Randy Herrington, dir., *Road House* (Silver Pictures, 1989).

of the doubt and extend grace to others until they prove that you shouldn't, and then treat them accordingly. For me, the simpler version of that quote is "Be kind."

For many people "kind" has become equivalent to "nice," when the complete opposite is true. Nice is offering sympathy when the neighbor has a flat tire, whereas kind is helping them change it. Nice is subjugating your own needs for friends and family because you don't want to be a bother. Kind is standing up for yourself. Nice wants to soothe things over, even when they are wrong. Kind stands firm against the ills of society. Nice is satisfied with keeping the status quo. Kind marches for the rights of those who still face oppression and inequality. Niceness is "love and light," a limiting belief in which we ignore our true power to make change and instead focus on the superficial. However, kindness is "fuck around and find out," in which we engage all our magical muscles to make change.

Nice is what you say, and kind is what you do.

At its most basic, nice is what you say, and kind is what you do.

Boundaries

Kindness means protecting your space and enforcing boundaries. You cannot work magic if your own self is a mess, mystically speaking. Regular shielding, grounding, and cleansing are all important, as well as knowing just what you are comfortable with in your practice. This is especially important if you start working with spirits and deities. Having a strong sense of self will keep you from being taken advantage of by those entities. As a witch, get into the practice of saying no. This might be especially hard if you are a people pleaser, but it is important because you need to guard your emotional, magical, and physical energies. If saying "no" feels too much for you to begin with, then work on shielding yourself, which is a metaphysical way of doing the same.

Shielding is a magical form of personal protection. It is simple enough to do: imagine a bubble of white light around your body. This energy forms a shield through which nothing magical can pass to get to you. You can play around with the energy, programming it so that it keeps out only unwanted magics. The shield can also work to keep malicious energies from attaching themselves to you. Visualizing the shield around you takes only seconds. Put it up right when you leave your house in the morning, before you enter a room full of people, or whenever else you think you will need to be protected.

Once you are comfortable with creating the boundaries around yourself, you should gain the confidence to do the same in other areas of your life. Being deliberate with where and how you spend your energy opens you up to new possibilities.

Kindness for Yourself

The thing about kindness is that we will often extend it to others before ourselves. We might also think that we are less deserving than others when it comes to a rich life. And that thought can infect our witchcraft when we do try to work magic to our own benefit. But kindness tells us that we are worthy of good things, safety, love, peace, and joy.

Self-doubt is one of the most insidious saboteurs of magic. We can gather together all our materials. We can time everything right. We can say the words perfectly, but if we doubt our abilities, if we are unkind to ourselves, our magic will be lacking. "Fake it till you make it" is common advice when it comes to this dilemma, the idea being that if you engage in acts of kindness to yourself, you will eventually come to view yourself through a lens of grace. That's all well and good, but I'm a witch—I prefer to find magical help for my problems. In this case, I find that binding my self-doubt does the trick.

A Binding Spell for Self-Doubt

This spell is best done in your astral residence, as it deals with your feelings. Enter your astral residence and start by creating a summoning circle. You can make this a variety of ways. Maybe you visualize laying down a circle of salt and herbs such as dandelion leaf, mullein, or wormwood. You can also draw the circle in a clockwise direction with light emanating from the pointer finger of your dominant hand. Make the circle so that you stand outside of it. However you do it, once you have created your summoning circle, it is time to call up your self-doubt. This is your own personal demon, so you can call it into the circle, where it will be stuck until you release it. Know that it cannot get out of the summoning circle to harm you.

Visualize the self-doubt as clearly as you can. Maybe it looks like a gremlin or a demon, or perhaps it manifests itself as an odor or a feeling of dread. You will know it by the way it feels to you when it appears. Now tell your self-doubt that you are binding it from affecting you. Affirm that you are a powerful witch who can work magic to your benefit because you deserve to have good things happen in your life. Tell the self-doubt that you are the one in control, not it. Put as much power and emotion behind the words as you can.

Once you have told off your self-doubt and established your control over it, it is time to bind it. Visualize the self-doubt being bound by chains, ropes, vines, white light, or however you want. See that it cannot break free from its bindings no matter how hard it struggles. Use your words to strengthen these bindings. Tell your self-doubt that your magic will keep it restrained.

Once it is bound, send the self-doubt away. I prefer to send mine to the vacuum of space, but you can visualize it being locked up in a chest, buried in the dark earth, sent into the sun, or any other place where it will not be able to easily escape. Stay a moment with the feeling of its absence from the summoning circle and from your body and mind. You are free. This can be a very emotional process. If the emotions that were brought up were negative, make sure to ground after you have worked this magic so that those feelings can be transformed into positive ones. If the emotions are positive, sit in them and feel their power wash over you.

Before you leave your astral residence, clean up the summoning circle. If you drew the circle with light, erase it with the pointer finger of your nondominant hand in a counterclockwise direction. If you used materia magica to make the circle, sweep up the materials and dispose of them. And then, once your astral residence has been set back to rights, return to your physical body, ready to cast spells for your own benefit.

You may need to repeat this spell a few more times for it to stick. Self-doubt is a wily trickster and knows many ways to escape bonds, but you are smarter than it and you can keep chaining it up until it finally withers and dies away.

What it comes down to is that kindness allows for a variety of responses to different situations. Instead of relying on being nice, we can evaluate our toolbox for the most appropriate reaction.

The Place of Compassion in Witchcraft

The late Terry Pratchett, in his Discworld series, gave us some of the best examples of witches in fiction. In his novel *Lords and Ladies*, a magical contest between two witches puts a child in danger. One of the witches ends the contest by backing down, thus saving the child but losing to the other witch. While the other witch claims victory, the townsfolk declare the one who stopped the contest to save the child as the winner. When the other witch objects, she is told, "This is not a contest about power…it is a contest about witchcraft. Do you even begin to know what being a witch *is*? Is a witch someone who would look round when she heard a child scream?" To which the entire town affirms, "Yes."[12]

Witches of centuries past were often healers, counselors, and advisors to those who came knocking on their doors. They provided information about the future, insight into the past, and assurances about the present. Even during the height of the witch hunts in Europe, people still consulted with witches about their everyday lives. And today, people still turn to witches for help through tarot readings, astrology, shadow work guidance, and more. All of this requires a certain amount of compassion for others.

If you are called upon to cast a spell for another, you'll need to approach the task with empathy. You cannot successfully cast magic to solve a problem if you don't understand it to begin with. This is where compassion can come into play. You need to spend time listening not only to what the other person wants but to their unspoken desires as well. Before you say yes to casting a spell for another, you need to know the scope of what will be involved. Sit down with the person and find out what it is that they want to accomplish and then decide if that is something you want to be a party to. Remember your boundaries. And know that it is okay to say no, if necessary. And should you decide that you will work magic for another, go through all the steps from page 42 in the

12. Terry Pratchett, *Lords and Ladies* (Harper Collins, 1996), loc. 95, Kindle.

"Creating Your Own Spells and Rituals" section just as you would for your own spellcrafting.

The Interconnectedness of the World

It isn't that great of a leap from seeing the interconnectedness of nature to the same in modern human society. Humans have the greatest impact on the world of any living organism, and our influence is negative at this point. It would be easy to devolve into misanthropic thinking when faced with that reality. But if we know that we are connected to each other just as with nature, compassion is not far behind.

A witch is mindful of those ties that bind people, places, and things together. Their magic casting can have unintended consequences if those connections aren't taken into account.

A few years ago, after it became apparent that my ex-husband was being emotionally abusive to our daughter, I was rightfully angry and considered hexing him. I refrained, however, because I didn't want there to be a blowback on her. Taking into account that the three of us were tangled together because I was co-parenting with him, I opted for a binding spell instead. I drilled down further with my intentions for the spell to target his behavior toward our daughter, instead of doing a general binding. As satisfying as it would have been to call on Nemesis, the Greek goddess of vengeance, or sic the Furies on him, it would not have been a kindness to my daughter. I had to put her welfare before my own thirst for vengeance.

Kindness, and the understanding that comes with it, informs the witch about the kind of magic to cast for each situation. It requires us to practice our craft deliberately and with an eye toward unintended consequences.

We are required to take a moment and consider what other results may come from our spellcasting and to limit the impact it might have on innocent bystanders.

This is where divination can help with spellcasting. This is why many tarot spreads include the question "What will be the outcome of my action(s)?" You can also meditate, reach out to your spirit helpers and deities for their input, or even just imagine the possible scenarios that might happen in response to your spellwork.

This desire to avoid unintended consequences of our magic can lead some witches to use the phrase "for the highest good of all and harm to none" as a way to head them off. This is fine for most spells, but if you are actively trying to harm another, it will, of course, then negate your spellwork. Instead, it's better to spend your time researching what the full consequences of your spell might be and then building in countermeasures to them. For example, if you are performing a money or riches spell, you want to be very specific about where and how the money will come to you to avoid things like getting it as an inheritance from the passing of your beloved aunt. That is a very dramatic example, but it highlights the importance of thinking your spells through before you cast them.

Protection Magic

Protection magic, cutting cords, setting boundaries, and calling back one's energy are all aspects of being kind to oneself. A witch knows that they must take care of themselves first before they can help others. They make it a regular practice to cleanse their energetic bodies and put up protective shields against malicious magics.

You should already be using a shielding technique to keep yourself protected from any stray, malicious, or negative energy that can attach itself to you. But you might find that you need to be a bit more proactive in your protection magic.

Kindness Is Not Karma

Karma is a term that gets thrown around in a lot of witchy circles. The idea that there is a cosmic scale that will balance out all the bad things that have happened to you is a comforting thought. The idea of the threefold law, that what you put out into the universe magically will come back to you three times over, is related to this idea of mystical justice. There are problems with these ideas, however. First, karma works on a larger scale than the day to day. It is a lifetime cycle and doesn't mean that the guy who cut you off in traffic will end up with a flat tire later because of his actions. The threefold rule, on the other hand, seems designed to restrict witches in their magic for fear of mystical backlash. Instead, I believe kindness means that it falls to us to balance the scales of justice. Sometimes the kindest thing you can do is make someone face the consequences of their actions.

Kindness is a worldview that is concerned with the well-being of people. This means being willing to call out bad behavior, as well as call in the folk who are behaving badly. It means extending grace to others and, just as importantly, to ourselves. It encompasses the qualities of compassion, equality, and justice. For the witch, kindness should always underpin their magic. It is not niceness that motivates a witch, but a kindness for the world as they want it to be.

And so, if you find yourself in a situation where you are called on to work greater magic for protection, or even to work magic against someone else, you should do so with great care. Start small. A binding or reversal spell might be all you need to address the situation. If you must do a bit of universal realignment, go through the process of figuring out all the consequences that might happen before you cast your magic. You don't want to have any innocent bystanders swept up in your magic.

A Reversal Spell

Use this spell if you need to reflect back to an individual their malicious intentions and energy. This spell is particularly useful when paired with a shielding spell so that the energies don't even reach you before they are bounced back.

You'll need:

- Small round mirror. You can use a compact or get a mirror from a craft store.
- Anointing oil made from rosemary essential oil and olive oil
- Small piece of paper and a pen if using a compact, or black permanent marker if using an unmounted mirror
- Small pouch of black fabric if you are using an unmounted mirror

Start by cleansing your space and cleansing the mirror. The best way to do this is to either wash the mirror with salt water or smoke cleanse it with an incense like frankincense, lavender, or cedar. Next, write the name of the person you are sending the energy back to either on the back of the mirror with the permanent marker or on the piece of paper. Using the rosemary anointing oil, draw a circle with a slash through it on the mirror with your fingertip. Say something along the lines of "Everything [name of the person] sends to me has no effect and gets reflected back to them."

Place the unmounted mirror in the black fabric pouch. If you are using a compact, place the piece of paper with the name on it into the compact and close it up. You can leave the mirror on your altar, store it in a dark, out-of-the-way place, or carry it on you if you have to deal with the person often. If the issue with the person ever is resolved and you are no longer in need of the spell, you can dispose of it. In this case, that means removing the paper from the compact and burning it. If you are using an unmounted mirror, you can smash the mirror and then bury the shards somewhere far from where you sleep.

When You Need to Curse

There may come a time when you need to curse someone. You have weighed all the options, you have tried the gentler approach to the situation, you have tried to work things out, and nothing has worked. It's time to pull out the pepper, lemon, pins, and needles. Before you curse someone, you need to make sure that you have done everything you can to narrow the scope of your spell. This means engaging in divination beforehand, looking at the possible ways it can backfire, and working to limit the blowback to unaffiliated parties.

The Sour Jar Spell

The effectiveness of this spell is directly proportional to the amount of energy and emotion you put into it. If you are feeling at all uncertain about cursing your victim, that's a sign you shouldn't do it. You should be full of conviction that this is your last resort and your target is truly deserving of having their life turned upside down. If you are positive on both accounts, then proceed.

You'll need:

- Photo of the person you are looking to curse. The photo should only show the person you are cursing, no one else.
- Pen
- Small piece of paper if you don't have a photo
- Knife
- Lemon
- Pins, needles, thorns, or twine
- Jar big enough to fit the lemon
- Black pepper
- Cayenne
- Red pepper flakes
- Salt
- Vinegar
- Black candle

Once you have your components, you want to cast some protection on yourself. A shielding spell will work. You are going to be working with powerful, toxic energies, and you don't want any of them attaching themselves to you. Visualize a bubble of white, protective light all around you to protect you.

Start with the photo. With a pen, cross out the eyes and mouth of the person. Say, "[Name of person] is cursed. May they never have rest. May they be plagued by all the same evils they visited upon me. May strife constantly follow them. May they never know peace or prosperity." You can also write this on the back of the photo to cement the sentiment and power of your words. If you don't have a photo, write the person's name on a piece of paper and write the same incantation on the paper. Fold the paper or the photo up, folding away from you three times.

Cut a deep slit in the lemon and slide the photo or piece of paper into the slit. Use the pins, needles, thorns, or twine to close the slit, sealing the photo or piece of paper in the lemon. Say, "May [name of person]'s life always be sour."

Place the lemon in the jar. Sprinkle on top of it the various peppers and salt. Use as much of each as you wish, but leave enough room to add the vinegar. Say, "May [name of person] always feel discomfort."

Fill the jar the rest of the way with the vinegar. Say, "May [name of person] always feel the sting of retribution."

Cap the jar and light the black candle. Dribble a little bit of wax in the middle of the jar lid and use that to affix the candle to the top of the jar. Let the candle burn all the way down. The wax should drip over the lid and down the jar, helping seal it.

Once the wax has hardened, give the jar a shake. As you do so, feed all your anger, frustration, hatred, and other negative emotions into the jar. Say, "May [name of person]'s life always be turbulent."

Feed all your negative emotions into the jar.

Keep the jar in a dark place for the next nine days. Each day shake it again, feeding your emotions into the jar and reminding it of its charge that the person's life should be turbulent and sour. After the ninth day, take the jar out somewhere far from where you sleep and bury it deep into the ground where it can continue to work its magic.

Afterward, take a cleansing bath and lay down your protections again. Remember to do the mundane work to support your curse. Avoid the person if possible, file a police report if necessary, learn self-defense, and continue to shield yourself. Know that you have given them the kindness of reaping what they have sown. Be at peace with yourself.

Kindness for yourself can be a difficult ask for many. We are so much more comfortable with extending kindness to others and leaving nothing for ourselves. But as you have seen, kindness needs to start with you. The saying goes "You can't pour from an empty cup," and this is just as true for mundane as magical concerns. Practicing kindness allows you to see the connections between you and the rest of the world. It is through those connections that you can work magic to protect yourself and others, hurt and heal. Remember that being kind does not mean being nice, and you have all the reasons in the world to protect your peace from those who would destroy it.

EXERCISES

This chapter's exercises are meant to help you find your connections, to yourself and others. Kindness starts at home, and so I ask you to spend a little time on introspection to better understand yourself and others.

Your Witchy Qualities

YOU'LL NEED:

- Your book of shadows (if you keep one), a few sheets of paper, or even the Notes app on your phone
- Something to write with

It's now time to show some kindness to yourself. You are going to write down things about yourself that you like. These can be anything, from your hobbies to your physical characteristics to your way of thinking to quirks or habits. The point is to think about yourself and write down all the good things about yourself.

This may be an uncomfortable or difficult exercise for some people, especially women, as we are often told by society that focusing on ourselves is vain and selfish. However, this self-knowledge is important for your magic. You need to be in touch with yourself in order to know what it is you need to practice your craft. Power through the discomfort and write at least three things that you can come up with. You can always come back to this list later on to add things that you think of.

Now take your list and turn it into a table of correspondences. List archetypes, tarot cards, herbs, and crystals that relate to the qualities you have written down. You will be turning your life and your body into a walking encyclopedia of your personal magical practice. For example, if you wrote down that you like your reading habits, you might associate that with the archetype of the Sage, the Hierophant tarot card, the sage plant, and lapis lazuli. So when you need to invoke wisdom and learning into your life, you can use any of those correspondences in your spellwork.

Take time to consider what these qualities you like say about you magically. Are many of your qualities rooted in your intellect? Are they more emotional-based? Are they physical aspects? This revelation can give you a clue to what sort of magic will provide the best results for you.

Your Connections

You'll need

- Your book of shadows (if you keep one), a few sheets of paper, or even the Notes app on your phone
- Something to write with

This exercise helps you explore your connections to various entities and objects. As we saw in this chapter, we are all interconnected. Being able to see those connections is an important ability for the witch. Not only will they then be better able to see the consequences of their spellcasting, but they will be able to see ways to use certain objects in their magic.

Start with the following question: "How are you and trees connected?" Write everything you can think of that connects you to trees. You can focus on trees in general or, even better, a particular tree you are familiar with. Move on from trees to the connections between you and worms, mushrooms, quartz crystals, angler fish, your neighbor, and your local politician. You can draw these connections instead of writing words if you wish, or even create a collage that works out the connections. Find out what you have common with each of these individuals.

Now that you have created the connections between yourself and the above, write down how you relate to them magically. Perhaps you use the tree for materia magica, or you can perform a sweetening spell on the politician to be more receptive to your policy proposal. Maybe you need to create a good neighbors spell for your neighborhood to deal with issues of trespassing. Find at least one bit of magic that ties you and that plant, mineral, animal, or person together.

This, again, helps you start rooting your magic into yourself. It also allows you to identify allies in your craft. Those items, spirits, deities, plants, and animals that you have stronger connections with can be called on to help fuel your magic.

A Witch Is Patient

When I told my husband that one of the chapters in *A Witch Is* was going to be about patience, he laughed. I am notoriously bad at being patient. I hate waiting as much as Inigo Montoya. And I will be the first to admit that this was one of the hardest lessons I had to learn as a witch. Modern media would have us believe that one only has to flourish a wand and say a few rhymes, and the magic happens instantaneously. That might make for good storytelling, but real magic has to contend with all sorts of obstacles and conditions to work, many of which are out of our control. So we must cast our spells with the confidence that it will work, and then wait for our results. The waiting can be very difficult.

But obsessing over our magic once we've cast it isn't helpful either. When we keep thinking of the spell we've cast, or of the results we're waiting for, we pull our intentions built into the magic back to us. It's like putting a leash on your spellwork. You jerk the line every time you think about the spell, which keeps it from doing its work. So how do you practice the art of patience when rent is due in six days and your car is broken down and your lover left you? First, you start by understanding why it is that magic takes time. Then, you remember to work magical timing into your spells when you cast them. You write down what it is that you are doing. And finally, you engage in various other activities that will keep your mind off your magic so it can accomplish the task you set it to do.

Magic Takes Time

While magic is a matter of our will and intentions, the universe is big, with billions of others working to manifest their own desires. Metaphors of webs and tapestries capture how entangled we are with others, although personally, I prefer to see magic as a reflection of nature. The bird who is going after the worm is also prey for the wild cat. Tree roots compete with each other for resources. Fungi spread and break down material that was once alive. Everything is in competition with everything else, and so it is with magic. You cast a spell for love, sending that energy out into the universe, where it is buffeted by some energies and stymied by others. It has to overcome obstacles in the shape of people who are already in relationships or otherwise unavailable for your love. That spell has to sort through all the potential lovers to find the few that fit your criteria and then deal with things like physical distance to bring the One into your orbit. Knowing all that, it is often easy to decide that magic can't work. Keeping in mind all that your magic has to go through to deliver results is the first step of cultivating the necessary patience for witchcraft.

I prefer to see magic as a reflection of nature.

It also helps to manage expectations. Once again, we have to contend with the media and the unrealistic expectations it has given us regarding magic. Magic, in fiction, can accomplish great things, seemingly without any effort on the part of the witch. However, in real life, the results can vary greatly. You may be able to cast a successful spell without doing any of the mundane work to support it. But it will take longer to work. Similarly, if you attempt to affect things that have no connection to you, it will take a long time to see results. In fact, by the time the magic has worked, or by the time you realize it hasn't, you may no longer need the result you were aiming for. In understanding the limits of your magic, you can do wonderful, powerful things. And you will be more confident in your spellcasting.

Later, in chapter 9, I'll talk more about what to include in your spells to ensure that they get results. However, one way you can help yourself in this area is to create deadlines for your spell to work. This way, you will know that if the spell hasn't seen results by a certain time, it didn't work and you won't be wasting your time waiting for something that isn't going to happen. You can then do divination to find out why the spell didn't work.

Keep in mind that while magic takes time, there are things you can do to help it along. Yes, doing the mundane support work is part of this. Going back to the spell for love example, you have to put yourself into situations where you can meet people, work on yourself so that you have something to bring to a relationship, and be open to what the magic you sent out brings into your orbit. Another way you can speed up results is by putting the spell out of your mind. Thinking about the spell constantly pulls the energy back to you and keeps it from doing its work. I'll get into more detail on what you can do while you're waiting later in this chapter.

For now, it's enough that you are aware that you have a hand in how fast, or slow, your magic works.

Another way you can help your spellcasting along is to take into account the time when you are casting your spells, which is the topic of the next section.

Magical Timing for Better Spellcasting

One of the foundations for witchcraft is magical timing. The idea is to tap into the energies of certain times of the year, month, week, and even day to help supercharge your spellwork. Using magical timing can help you feel more in tune with the seasons and thus amplify your magic.

Now, while magical timing can help enhance your spellwork, you shouldn't hold yourself to it at all times. If you need to do a spell right this minute, you do the spell, timing of the moon phase be damned. Magical timing is not for spontaneous spellcasting. It is for those spells on which you want to take your time.

Many witches focus on the phases of the moon when determining their spell timing. It's popular because it requires no special equipment to determine what phase the moon is in—just go outside at night and look. It happens at regular intervals, which means that you can set up monthly spells without having to wait for a very long time. And the moon provides potent energies for every kind of spell depending on its phase. When in doubt, you can't go wrong with performing just about any kind of spell during the full moon.

Waiting for a moon phase might not be desirable, however, which is where the days of the week and the hours of the day come into play. Over time, each day of the week has been assigned its own lore and energies determined by various factors, such as who the day is named after and the modern arrangement of days on the calendar. So, for example, Wednesday is named for Woden, whose Greek and Roman counterparts are Hermes and Mercury, respectively. These gods are associated with messages, which is why Wednesday is often said to be good for spells dealing with communication, travel, and self-expression. Because it is considered the middle of the work week on the modern calendar, it is also a good day to perform spells for overcoming obstacles (due to it being known as "hump day").

Drilling down further, each hour of the day is associated with a planet. This covers the classical planets, so the moon and sun are included along with Mercury, Venus, Mars, Jupiter, and Saturn. Each of these planetary associations gives the hours of the day certain energies that can be tapped into for magic. Planetary hours are calculated not only by when the sun rises and sets, but also based on where one is when making the calculation. The calculations involve finding how many minutes pass between the rising and the setting of the sun and then dividing that number by twelve. To figure out the nightly planetary hours, you find how many minutes pass between the setting of the sun to the rising of it the following day, and then again divide it by twelve. Then you assign the planetary hours, starting with the planet that rules the particular day you are calculating, and following the cycle of Mercury, Moon, Saturn, Jupiter, Mars, Sun, Venus.

It gets even more complicated when taking into account other factors, which are beyond the scope of this brief section. Fortunately, you don't need to do the math yourself, as there are calculators online that can do it for you. Websites like Planetary Hours (planetaryhours.net) and apps like Planetaro will calculate the hours for you.

What the differing hours give you is the chance to time your magic to an hour that best supports the magic you are attempting.

This gives you even greater flexibility, as there are multiple times throughout the day for each planetary hour. Thus, if you are casting a spell that needs sensual or romantic energies, you can look up when the next Venus planetary hour is and cast your spell then.

There are more obscure timings that you can take advantage of as well. The parts of the day (morning, noon, and night) correspond to the phases of the moon (waxing, full, and waning) but are associated with the sun. There are also astrological events, such as eclipses, solstices, and equinoxes that provide other opportunities for added energy to spellcasting.

If you want to get particularly fancy with your spellcasting, you can combine all these magical timing factors for one spell. If you are casting a spell for health, for example, you could choose a date and time that sees a full moon falling on a Sunday, Monday, or Friday, during planetary hours ruled by the sun or Mars. Breaking out a calendar and looking ahead should give you at least one day that fits the bill. You would then cast your spell at that time, on that day, to receive the maximum boost to your spell.

Taking the time to work out the magical timing of your spell helps you refine and focus what your intentions are. Continuing with the health spell as an example, you'll see that it could be worked on Sunday, Monday, or Friday. Each one of those days is associated with healing and health, but they are also associated with other energies. Sunday is often associated with general healing, whereas Monday is associated with healing as well as internal issues such as emotions. So if your healing is targeting your mental health, you might want to use Monday instead of Sunday. Drilling down even further, say you need an aggressive form of healing. Tapping into the planetary energies of Mars when choosing the hour you'll cast your spell on a Sunday can give your spell a boost.

You can also use magical timing in determining the deadline for your spell. Choose a day or planetary hour that makes your spell start and end with a bang. Using Sunday is a good choice, as it is associated with the sun, victory, and success.

If you do include magical timing in your spellwork, make sure to mark it down so that you will have an accurate record of how long the spell took and what energies you added to it via timing. In fact, writing down everything about your spell so that you can refer back to it later is a very good idea.

Write It All Down

Adam Savage, of *MythBusters* fame, has a saying: "Remember kids, the only difference between screwing around and science is writing it down."[13] This advice, I have found, applies just as much to magic as to science. History is filled with examples of magic books. From scrolls and lead tablets, to grimoires and codices, to the witchcraft books you find on the shelf at your local bookstore, magic and writing have always been intertwined.

I'm a big proponent of keeping notes on your magic, whether that be in a journal, a book of shadows, a planner, or some other form of record. Personally, I have a journal that covers the whole year. In it I keep not only my personal, mundane thoughts, tasks, and appointments but also the magical ones. Since I see very little space between my magical and mundane life, it makes sense for me to keep everything in one place. The benefit of this is that I

13. *MythBusters*, season 10, episode 8, "Bouncing Bullet," aired May 13, 2012, on Discovery Channel.

have a place I can consult when I am curious about the results of my magic. This can be helpful to you as well.

Keeping a record of your magical efforts can show you what has worked and what hasn't. It allows you to troubleshoot your magic and also see where you have had successes, which will boost your magical self-confidence. Additionally, keeping a record is a way to acknowledge that you are a witch. You are doing this magic thing, and you are doing it your way. It also allows you to keep track of any changes you made to spells that you cast from other sources, what the magical timing was, how long it took to see results, and so much more.

To start your own journal or book of shadows, you need only a notepad and a writing utensil. You can also keep your journal on your phone or computer. It is more important to choose a method you will keep up with than to pick one you think is "witchy." Consider your lifestyle and your day-to-day schedule when deciding the way you'll be keeping your journal. Paper requires you to have some time to write, whereas the Notes app on your phone might be more readily available if you are anything like most people who keep their phone on hand throughout the day. If you choose a paper journal but don't want to carry a bulky one around with you, opt for the small memo-size journal that can easily fit in pockets.

While your notebook doesn't need to be fancy, you can glam it up with stickers, transfers, stencils, and more if you want. The same goes for images that you can add to your digital files. Sometimes it can help inspire you to write when you have a magical tool on hand. The important point is to take time to play around with styles and layouts to find your perfect journal format. You may start off with the Notes app on your phone and later decide to switch to a leather-bound journal. That's perfectly fine. Just transfer your previous notes over. If you decide to go digital, use your phone's camera or a scanner to digitize your paper pages so that you'll have access to them later.

Once you have a journal setup that works for you, start writing down what you are doing when you cast your spell. Note the spell timing, the components, how you were feeling when you cast the spell, what words were used, what happened—every detail that you can think of. You can do this either after casting the spell or during it, if you have breaks for recording built in. You want to note anything that seems important to you so that when you come back to the entry later, you will be able to understand the nitty-gritty of what you did.

Once you have written down what you did, you can let the entry sit, just like you are letting your spell work without micromanaging it. You don't want to obsess over what you wrote. It's there for you to consult later. You can consult the entries when you are worried the spell isn't working, to troubleshoot what happened, or to record the results.

When you start to see results, or when you are certain the spell failed, go back to the entry and write down what happened to make you think so. This is where including deadlines in your spell can be helpful, as you know when you should be seeing results. Be as detailed in your follow-up entry as you were with the original. Include things like how you felt since you cast the spell, any signs you might have seen indicating success or failure, and anything unusual that happened since you cast the spell.

If the spell didn't work, you can use the entry to go over why you think that happened. As you go on recording your spells, you may be able to pick up on trends or commonalities. Maybe whenever you use a certain herb or crystal in your spells, they fail. Or maybe you find that spells cast on the new moon work well for you. By keeping records, you can find those things that help you build a better, personal practice that works every time.

Finally, consulting past entries can help you when you can't get your current spellwork out of your mind. Looking at past successful magic will reaffirm that you can accomplish great things through magic. Focusing on your successes will increase your confidence that this spell will succeed as well. To help with this, make sure to mark those entries that saw results so that they are easier to find. Don't look at any entries of spells that failed or at the current spells that are working away in the background. These will just drag you down into self-doubt, and that's not what you need to be feeling right now.

While You Are Waiting

Waiting can be the hardest part of working magic. We tend to obsess over our spellwork. We always want to check in, to get assurances that our magic worked. It can be hard to accept that we have to relinquish control and trust in the magic when one of the allures of that same magic is the ability to take control of the world around you. There is, of course, a difference between thinking about the spell and obsessing over it. If your spell has physical components to it, such as a spell pouch, spell jar, or the like, your mind will touch upon the spell every time you look at it. This is different from constantly worrying about if the spell is working, wondering when you will see results, or fretting over the outcome of your magic. If you find yourself spending longer than a second or two thinking about your spell, you may be bogging it down. It's important to know the difference so that you can take measures to mitigate any interference originating from your own self.

There are ways you can work around obsessing over your spell. If you can distract yourself, that is great. Move on to the next thing, read a book, watch a movie, walk, garden, cook, or dance, whatever will shift your focus away from the magic. Mundane tasks, which take you as far away from magic as possible, help in this regard.

It's much easier to talk about keeping your mind off your spellwork than to accomplish it. This is where creating rituals and habits will help you. Often, when you are meditating, there will be a time at the end of the meditation when you are told to come back to your body. You need to wiggle your toes and fingers and bring your consciousness back to the physical. This is a finishing ritual, one that sends a signal to your brain that you are no longer meditating. Similarly, when you engage in spellwork, if you create sacred space, such as a circle, you need to dismiss that space once the spell has been cast or the ritual has ended. You can do the same when you cast a spell to signal to your mind that you aren't going to think about it any longer. You can imagine closing a door behind your spell as it goes out into the universe. Or you can build an activity into the back end of the spell, such as taking a walk or engaging in a mundane task once you've finished the spell. The point is to get your body and mind out of magic mode so that you can forget what it is that you have done.

Decide ahead of time on your ending action for spellwork.

If you decide ahead of time on your ending action for spellwork, it is more likely that you will do it regularly. Then you can work it into your spell routine when you are creating your own spells and rituals. Choose an activity that you are most likely to do. Even something as simple as drinking a glass of water after casting a spell will work—and keep you hydrated!

If you find you can't do that, focus on helping the magic along. If you have done a spell for employment, for example, polish up your résumé, apply for jobs, create a LinkedIn profile, and network. Magic follows the path of least resistance, and if you can lay the groundwork mundanely, that aids in the spellwork.

For example, in 2017, I decided to try to find a publisher for my book *Sew Witchy*. I started off with a spell to land a contract. To aid the spell, I researched publishers and wrote a proposal. I sent that off to my first choice of publisher on Valentine's Day. And then I went back to my work as a sewist. I could have stopped at the spell, but the likelihood that a contract would fall in my lap was small. I still had to do the work. And once I was done, I had to put the whole endeavor out of my mind. It was easier for me at this time, as I was still struggling to make ends meet, and constantly hitting refresh on my email wasn't going to help with that. By the time I heard back from the publisher with an offer for a contract, I had completely forgotten about sending off the proposal in the first place.

Journaling or meditating can help keep your mind focused on the results, rather than if the spell working behind the scenes. You can write around the spell by focusing on the way your life will be impacted when you achieve the results you are working toward. What will your life look like? What will you do when you succeed? How will you feel? In this case, you are imagining that the spell has already worked and you are now benefiting from it. Write as if it has succeeded and what your next steps are. Focusing on the future will put you into the mindset of already having accomplished what you set out to do, which will trick your mind into not thinking about the spell.

What if you do all that but still find yourself thinking about your spellwork, impatient to see results? It's time for a little mental jujitsu to make that nervous energy work for you. Mat Auryn, author of *Psychic Witch*, suggests using affirmations when you find yourself obsessing.[14] So, returning to our job spell example, you would affirm "I am abundant" or "Money flows to me easily" or something similar whenever your mind is drawn to the spell. That is another way of lighting beacons to guide the way of the magic without calling its energy back to you.

This can be one of the most difficult lessons to learn in *A Witch Is*. We all want our magic to work right away, just like…well, magic. That is often the allure of magic, the promise of instant gratification and results. Which can mean it is frustrating when the magic doesn't work the way we want it to. Magic adheres to its own timeline, however, and the more we try to rush it, the more the magic will resist. That doesn't mean you can't do things that will help your magic to work on a timeline that better suits your needs. But it does mean that you must be deliberate and then willing to wait while your magic does the work. Work your timing, write down what you are doing, and then forget about your spellwork to give it the best chance of working.

In the end, patience is a trait that must be cultivated. Exercises like grounding and meditation can help you in that area. Grounding when you feel anxious about the spell you cast can help you push those nervous energies out of your body and into the earth, where they can be transmuted into calm. Breathing meditations, in which

14. Mat Auryn, "Mind Magick" panel, Between the Worlds/Sacred Space Conference, April 7, 2023.

you are aware of your breathing, can help clear your mind. As you breathe and thoughts or emotions rise up, competing for your attention, you acknowledge the thoughts and then let them drift away like bubbles. Focusing on your breathing allows you to clear your mind of the doubts and tension that come from wondering if your spell will work.

Practice both grounding and breathing techniques whenever you feel the urge to "check in" on your spell. They can take as little as thirty seconds and can greatly improve your mood.

Magical Timetables

YOU'LL NEED:

- Paper calendar or the calendar app on your phone (whichever one you use)
- Something to write with

If you wish to incorporate magical timing into your spellcasting, you'll need to be aware of when astrological events are occurring. There are plenty of different calendars on the market that track things like the movement of the planets, the moon phases, and events like the solstices and eclipses. There are also apps that do the same. For this exercise, you are going to add some of these magical timings to your calendar.

Start with the moon phases. Mark the new moon and full moon dates for the upcoming months on your calendar. Next, mark the solstices and equinoxes on your calendar. Finally, find out if there are any major astrological events that will be happening in the coming months. Look for things like eclipses, planetary retrogrades, and when the days move from one zodiac sign to the next. Fill out at least three months of your calendar with this information so that you have it all on hand.

Now that you have this information, you can start working it into your spellcasting. Consult your calendar when you are working out the details for your next spell and see if there are any upcoming events that might benefit your spell. Look to time your magic to the phases of the moon. Do some experiments, casting small spells including magical timing, and see which ones produce the best results. The benefit of this exercise is that it gets you thinking about broader connections between your magic and the world around you, allowing you to better hone your spells to see greater results.

Spell Aftercare

YOU'LL NEED:

- Your book of shadows (if you keep one), a few sheets of paper, or even the Notes app on your phone
- Something to write with

It is easier to engage in a ritual if you have an idea beforehand of what you are going to do. This is also true for what you do after the ritual or spell. In this exercise, you are going to put together a plan for how you will spend your time after casting a spell so that you'll be ready to do so the next time you work a spell. You want to focus on two areas when creating your aftercare steps: signaling the return to the mundane after spending so much time around magic and returning to your body.

For those witches who cast a circle or sacred space before they work magic, signaling the return to the mundane is as simple as removing the circle or closing the sacred space. If you don't do either, you can add a final step to your spellcasting to accomplish the same end. It doesn't have to be an elaborate or fancy action. Anything like ringing a bell, stating a phrase like "So mote it be," or blowing out a candle can signal the end of the spell or ritual. The point is to mark a clear end to the spell or ritual in a way that you understand. Try a few different actions until you find the one that feels right, and then incorporate it into your spellwork.

Once you have ended the spell, you want to get back into your body. Casting magic involves so many of our senses and energies that we need to call them back once we are done. For many witches, this can be as simple as eating or drinking something. For others, it might involve taking a shower, grounding and centering themselves, going for a walk, or other physical activities that remind them of their physical form. Think about what you could reasonably accomplish after casting your spell. Try out different actions until you find the one that fits your personality and abilities.

Write down what you have worked out for your aftercare ritual. Now that you have decided how you will end your spells and how you will reacquaint yourself with your physical body, make sure to implement both in your next spellcasting.

A Witch Is Intuitive

Intuition is a word that gets mentioned often without elaboration of its meaning. When witches talk about intuition, they are referencing knowing something innately without a conscious reason. It is an instinct that whispers answers to us that we might otherwise not know. It is a "gut feeling" that warns us of danger even when our rational minds don't see anything to worry about. In all these definitions, you'll notice the emphasis is on feelings rather than logic. With today's society's promotion of abstract thought over emotional intelligence, we often dismiss our intuition as not real. But to ignore it is to lose access to a powerful tool for magic.

Intuition is especially important when it comes to witchcraft, as it can help us make decisions faster than our logical brain can put together information. Intuition also deals with non-mundane information. When we consult divination, pay attention to our dreams, and meditate, we are tapping into knowledge that has no basis in rational thought.

While intuition is described as an instinct, that doesn't mean you can't cultivate it. There are several different ways you can do so. You can start by building trust in your body's signals. You then move on to practicing exercises to sharpen your intuition. Paying attention to your dreams and engaging in divination will also help you strengthen your intuitive abilities.

Trusting Your Gut

When it comes to intuition, a lot of the metaphors and descriptions refer to a physical reaction. It's a "gut feeling" or a "feeling of unease." You might feel the hairs stand up on your arms, or you might experience a cooling sensation on your skin. Your heart might beat a bit faster. All these physical changes indicate that your intuition is trying to tell you something. But if you aren't in tune with your body, you might miss those signs. Scanning your body and performing grounding exercises will help you better know your body and how it feels during different times.

Scan Your Body

Before you can understand what your body is saying, you need to know what is going on in it. Doing regular body scans can help you get better acquainted with your physical self. You want to engage in scans during different times so that you can know what your body is like when it is relaxed or tense. That will help you in noticing the differences in your body during different states.

A body scan is simply taking a mental note of parts of your body. You want to notice if the body part has any tension, pain, or stress or if it is calm and relaxed. To start, you can lie down, but you should be able to work your way to doing the scan when you are seated or standing. Once you've gotten into practice, doing a full body scan should only take a few seconds.

Lie, sit, or stand in a comfortable position. You don't want to put any strain on your body, as that will show up in your scan. Bring your attention to your toes. How do they feel? Is there any tension or pain there? You can wiggle them if you wish to help bring your attention to them. Next, bring your attention to the tops and soles of your feet. Again, look for any tension. Get a good feel for if they are relaxed and what that feels like. Move up to your ankles, then your calves, hips, and pelvis, and up through your body until you reach the top of your head.

Don't try to do anything about any tension or stress you find in your body as you go. This is a scan to diagnose how you feel. Later, you can do something about that, but now you just want to acknowledge the state of your body. Once you've reached the top of your head, the scan is complete. Do this scan several times during the first few days. Try it at night and first thing in the morning when you are lying in bed. This can give you a baseline to work with, as you should be at your most relaxed state when doing the body scan.

If you deal with chronic pain, your baseline will be different from the baseline of those who do not. That is okay. You know your body better than anyone else and will know when the pain you feel every day is different during the scan. The important point about this exercise is that you are building a mental map of what your body is like when it is as calm and relaxed as it possibly can be, so you will know when your intuition is speaking up through it.

Doing a body scan frequently will get you used to the feel of your body when it is in a non-intuitive state, which will make it more likely that you will be aware when your body sends signals that something is up.

Grounding

What if you can't get to a baseline because you suffer from anxiety disorders or otherwise can't get a read on your body? Then it is time to give your body a good emotional and energetic cleansing. For this, you want to ground (see page 6).

After grounding, go through the body scan. You should find it easier to now sense your baseline. Again, once you've been practicing both of these actions for a while, you should find that you can do both in less than thirty seconds. You should practice them at least once a day, to maintain an awareness of how you are doing physically.

When Your Body Speaks

Usually, when intuition kicks in, it makes itself known to you through a positive or negative sensation. When you've gotten used to how your body feels in its "default" state, you are better able to know when that intuitive sense kicks in. Now is the time to listen when your body is telling you something.

Listen when your body is telling you something.

The first thing to do when you feel that intuitive sense is to make note of it. Once you have become familiar with how your intuition manifests, you'll be faster at recognizing it. But in these first few instances, you really need to pause and reflect. What is the sensation you are feeling? Is it positive or negative? Where is it manifesting in your body?

Once you've noted the physical sensation, you can now focus on what your intuition is trying to tell you. If it is a positive feeling, that would indicate that you should do something. If it is negative, that indicates you should stop doing something or avoid a situation. Of course, that is a general description, and your decision will depend on the exact circumstances of the situation. Based on what your intuition says, you can then act on it.

You can also check in with your intuition, rather than waiting for it to make an appearance. To do so, ask your intuition a question and then see how it responds. It will speak up using the same physical sensations that you are used to experiencing when it pops up unbidden.

Now that you know what it feels like when your intuition is active, you can engage in various activities to sharpen it.

Sharpening Your Intuition

Intuition involves the feeling, creative side of your brain. Exercises like journaling, doodling, and meditation can help you tap into that part of your brain. Doing so while actively trying to engage your intuitive sense will help you recognize when it is speaking to you at other times. This is also where you can use your astral residence, which I discussed on page 49, to help cultivate your intuition. The astral residence gives you a safe place to connect with your emotional side and work some magic to help increase the connection between your conscious and subconscious.

Before you undergo this exercise, take the time to set the stage for success. Make sure you won't be disturbed by family, friends, or pets. Turn off any notifications that might interrupt you. Wear loose, comfortable clothes. You might make yourself a cup of mugwort or blue lotus tea or burn some rosemary or lavender incense. All of these aren't necessary, but they can help you get into the right frame of mind.

Start by going to your astral residence in the way that you usually do, whether this is through the staircase method or another. When you are inside, take a few moments to check the protections you have put in place on it. If necessary, reinforce the protections. If there is any maintenance that needs to be done, do it now. I always spend a few minutes cleaning and cleansing my space before I begin any magical work in my astral residence. Not only does this ensure that the space is ready for my work, but it gets me in a magical mindset.

Once you have done any pre-spell work, it is time to work on your intuition. To do so, you will first need to know where your intuition manifests. This is something you should have learned when doing body scans and paying attention to the feelings in your body, as discussed in the previous section. Bring your awareness to that portion of your body. Visualize your intuition as a swirling sphere of white and blue light. Examine the sphere. Are there any cloudy bits? Is it covered in cobwebs, or are there dark spots? Maybe it is a little dusty. This is an indication that your intuition is being underutilized or blocked. If so, you'll need to cleanse it.

To do so, visualize pulling white light or energy from the air around you and feeding it into the sphere. Your astral residence resides in your mind, where your subconscious and conscious meet, so the energy there is already attuned to your intuitive needs. Continue to pull and feed the energy into the sphere until all the spots, dullness, or dust are cleared away.

Now it's time to grow your intuition. Visualize the sphere growing larger as it swirls inside your body. The light from it fills your body, from the top of your head to the ends of your toes. As you do this, charge your intuition by saying this affirmation: "My intuition always leads me to what is right for me." You want to create the idea in your mind that not only is your intuition a tool that works for you, but it is also prevalent in your body, so that its messages come through loud and clear.

Once your body is filled with the intuitive light and energy, you can consult with your intuition over any current issues. Think about the issue at hand in great detail and then ask your intuition what you should do. Sit quietly and wait for the answer to come to you. It might come in the form of images or words, or it might just be an emotional response. The answer might come as a whisper or simply a gut feeling. No matter how it comes, however, give it time to fully address your question. After the answer comes, thank your intuition and let the light and energy fade back into the original sphere.

When you are done, leave your astral residence and return to your body. You might want to journal about what you learned. Return to your astral residence whenever you feel like you need to cultivate your intuition. After a while, you should be able to consult with it without having to meditate, journal, or use your inner mind as a conduit. The more you get in touch with your intuitive sense, the easier it will be to get answers.

Pay Attention to Your Dreams

Our subconscious is the gateway to our intuition. This is never as apparent as when we look to our dreams. The dreaming brain brings us messages and information that our logical, conscious brain misses in the hustle and bustle of waking life. With that in mind, paying attention to your dreams is one of the best ways to cultivate your intuition.

All you need to do so is restful sleep and a dream journal. The journal can be dedicated solely to your dreams, or it could be your book of shadows (if you keep one) or even just the Notes app on your phone. The important thing is that you have a place to write down your dreams when you wake up. This is an exercise that you need to engage in on a regular basis in order to increase your intuition. Make the decision to keep a dream journal for the length of a full moon cycle to get yourself into the habit.

To set yourself up for successful dreaming, make sure you have a good sleep routine. This means doing the same thing each night before going to bed and engaging in habits that encourage you to sleep. You can also add a magical boost to your sleep through the strategic use of crystals and herbs. Drinking a simple cup of mugwort tea or placing dried mugwort in a pouch under your bed can help with bringing on dreams, including prophetic ones. Use lavender and jasmine essential oils in a bed clothes spray to encourage restful sleep. You can also bring plants such as peace lilies or pothos into your bedroom to help clear the air for better breathing.

Keeping a piece of moonstone near your bed will help promote not only peaceful sleep but also lucid dreaming. Tiger's eye can increase the intensity of dreams and is helpful if you have difficulty remembering them. Clear quartz can also help in gaining clarity when it comes to the messages from your dreaming mind. You can place one or all three of these stones in a pouch to keep under your pillow.

Finally, you can use affirmations to inform your dreaming brain that you are open to whatever messages it conveys. A simple affirmation of "I receive wisdom from my dreams" can be enough. This sets the intention that you will receive messages from your dreams and that you will remember them to write them down.

Dreams are intimately personal in ways that many other things aren't. There are agreed-upon meanings of tarot cards, runes, and so on. Even language is a collection of sounds whose definition the community has, mostly, agreed upon. Dreams, however, happen in the private sphere of our minds, and while there are numerous books and websites that have definitions of symbols and images, they are often useless for any real, meaningful interpretation.

Think about houses in dreams, for example. Depending on the house, the meaning will be different for each person. In fact, you might dream of different houses, and each will have a separate meaning. My own dreams involve several different homes, and each has a distinct message for me. I know that if I dream of the house I grew up in, issues from the past will be coming up. However, if I dream of my grandparents' old house, I know there is a message about my ideal future for me to pay attention to. These interpretations didn't come to me immediately. It took a few years of cataloging and thinking on my dreams to figure out my own dream language.

It won't take you as long if you dedicate a few minutes each day to writing down your dreams when you wake up. This can take as little as five minutes and be done while you are still in your bed. You want to note any images from your dream and any emotional reaction you had to them. Don't worry if your dreams don't make sense to your waking mind; just record whatever you remember. Writing without editorializing is part of the process.

You can go further by spending a few more minutes journaling about what you dreamed:

- Were there any sensations in the dream other than just sight?
- What did you hear?
- Were there people you recognized in your dream?

- What is your relationship to those people in your waking life?
- What comes to mind when you think of the places that popped up in your dream?

Do similar themes, images, places, or people continue to pop up in your dreams? These can be building blocks of your personal dream language. Take note of them and what they might mean to you.

Try to keep in mind what you dreamed, especially what you felt, as you go about your day. If similar emotions pop up, pay attention to them and what is triggering them. This could be a pointer to the dream message your subconscious was sending you. At the end of the day before you go to bed, go back over your morning dream journal entry and see if anything that occurred in your dream can be related to what happened to you during the day.

If you do this regularly for at least a month, you should start to see an increase in your intuition and your ability to understand your personal dream language.

Divination

Humans have used divination for thousands of years to get answers that are not readily available by rational means. From watching the movement of birds to reading tarot, divination methods provide a direct line to our subconscious. This makes divination an effective tool for tapping into your intuition.

While one of the most popular forms of divination in witchy circles is tarot cards, they aren't always the best form to use when it comes to giving your intuition a medium. The benefit of tarot cards is that standard meanings have been worked out over centuries of use. This is useful in many situations but can also hamper your divination if you are relying on those meanings. Instead, tools such as tasseomancy (reading tea leaves) and scrying can provide you with better opportunities for intuitive divination. This is because they require you to tap into your subconscious mind to see the answers they provide.

Tasseomancy

The art of reading tea leaves has as long and storied a history as tea itself. The practice involves using loose-leaf tea. The answers come from the interpretation of the shapes found in the leaves. And while tasseomancy refers to tea-leaf reading, there are related forms of this type of divination that involve wax and ink.

To read the leaves, you will need a cup and a saucer as well as a loose-leaf tea blend. Don't use tea from a tea bag, as the tea is ground too fine to make the necessary clumps for reading. Let the tea steep and then drink it. During the process of brewing and drinking the tea, focus on your intention and question. As with most divination methods, specific, open-ended questions are better than general, yes-or-no questions. You want to concentrate on what you want to know. Let the warmth, scent, and taste of the tea help you achieve a relaxed and receptive state.

When you have finished the cup, swirl the dregs a couple of times, and then invert the cup onto the saucer. Leave the cup upside down for a moment, giving the excess liquid time to drain off the inside of the cup. Then turn the cup right-side up and observe the tea leaves that stick to its bottom and sides.

This is where your intuition comes in. Let your gaze soften as you look at the tea leaves. Make note of any shapes you see. Don't judge as you look. Let the first thing that comes to mind be your guide to how you interpret the shapes formed by the tea leaves.

These can give you insight into what is going on with the situation, as well as your own personal reaction to it.

Write down what you saw in the tea leaves and journal about it. Consider what the images you saw mean to you. What was your emotional reaction to what you saw? How might that relate to the situation you were asking about? Again, don't let your internal editor interfere with your interpretations. That is your conscious mind trying to make sense of something that goes beyond rational thought.

If tea drinking isn't your thing, you can engage in the same divination exercise by reading the shapes that ink or wax make in a bowl of water. For this, you need a bowl of cool water. You can add some moon water to it if you wish to help aid the process along. Then you'll need a candle or a dropper of India ink. Light the candle while you think about the situation you want clarity on. Drip wax from the candle into the water and interpret the shapes the wax makes. If you are using ink, let a few drops of the ink fall into the water and interpret the shapes the ink makes.

In both instances, you will again let your gaze soften and then open yourself to your intuition as you look at the shapes. Note down what you see and journal about it. Perform this exercise often, and you'll start to build your own personal dictionary of symbols you find in the shapes. Combining this with the symbolism you find in your dreams will give you the means for deeper understanding of yourself and your own magic. You can then start to bring this understanding to other forms of divination to get a truly personalized experience.

Scrying

Scrying involves looking at something—a mirror, a crystal ball, flames—and interpreting the images and shapes you see. This is the ultimate form of intuitive divination, as you are tapping directly into your visualization for answers to questions you have. Unlike tarot cards, which provide ready-made images, or tasseomancy, which provides shapes to interpret, scrying gives back only what you put into it.

If you are just starting out in scrying, I suggest working with flame scrying to begin. It provides a focal point for you to concentrate on and requires nothing more than a lit candle. To fire scry, light a candle, preferably a taper, and set it about twelve inches away from your face at a height where you can look at the flame comfortably.

Soften your gaze as you look at the flame. Concentrate on the situation you want insight into as you do so. Let all other thoughts fall away as you watch the way the flame flickers and moves. Make note of any images, feelings, or thoughts about the situation that start to come to mind as you watch the flame. This is your intuition speaking to you through the fire. After a moment, look away and then write down what you experienced. Journal about it, exploring how what you saw and felt relates to the question or situation you were asking about.

Scrying is the ultimate form of intuitive divination.

If you want to try mirror scrying, there are plenty of places where you can buy a scrying mirror, or you can make your own. To make your own scrying mirror, all you need is a picture frame and black paint. Remove the glass from the picture frame and paint one side of it black. When the paint is dry, return the glass to the frame, with the painted side facing in.

To use the scrying mirror, you'll need a candle and a slightly darkened room. Light the candle and set it off to the side of the mirror so that the light is indirectly reflected in the glass. Let your gaze soften and concentrate on the question or situation you want insight into. Keep your question open-ended and specific to get the best answers. General questions will get you general answers that might not be helpful.

Take note of any images, emotions, or thoughts that come up as you gaze into the mirror. Try not to editorialize as you stare in the mirror. Instead, just accept things as they come. After a few minutes, look away from the mirror and snuff out the candle. Write down what you saw and journal about it. This self-reflection is an important part of the process, as it gives you time to interpret what you saw and experienced.

Divination is a powerful tool in cultivating your intuition. The symbols circumvent our conscious mind and tap directly into our subconscious. Because it is a "witchy" activity, our critical mind will often check out so that we don't feel so pressured to come up with answers. That freedom allows us to be open and receptive to answers that aren't "logical" or based on reasoning. It can open us up to the greater wisdom of the universe, or at the very least get us thinking outside of the box to come up with unique answers to the situations we face every day.

 EXERCISES 

We often think of intuition as something someone is born with. But anyone can hone their intuitive sense. All it takes is paying attention to the changes in our body and to the personal symbolism that speaks to us every day. The following exercises are meant to help you cultivate your intuition through creating your own personal oracle to consult and by taking a look at a traditional form of divination and giving it your own spin.

Intuition Journal

YOU'LL NEED:

- Your book of shadows (if you keep one), a few sheets of paper, or even the Notes app on your phone
- Something to write with

In this exercise, you are going to keep an intuitive journal. For the span of a full moon cycle (from new moon to new moon), you will keep note of times when your intuition is speaking to you. This includes keeping track of your dreams, when you noticed your intuition speaking up, when you engaged in divination, and when you meditated. You don't need anything fancy; a small memo notebook or the Notes app on your phone will work just fine.

At the end of the moon cycle, go over your notes and mark out any recurring symbols, emotions, and thoughts that happened over the past twenty-eight days. I like to use a highlighter and go through the writing to first highlight anything that stands out. Then I can go back and consider what they might mean.

By keeping this journal and marking down when you have intuitive thoughts, you are not only building your own vocabulary but also strengthening your intuition by being aware when it speaks up. When signs appear, you will be able to recognize them.

Personal Interpretations in Tarot

YOU'LL NEED:

- Your book of shadows (if you keep one), a few sheets of paper, or even the Notes app on your phone
- Something to write with
- Tarot deck

I've mentioned before that one of the main benefits of the tarot is that standard meanings for each card have been worked out over centuries. Different decks might have their own slant on those standard meanings, but they will adhere to the general definitions. This means that the Magician will usually mean the same thing, no matter what deck you use. However, this often precludes intuitive readings, as people get stuck on those traditional meanings and don't dig deeper.

For this exercise, you are going to take the major arcana and start to connect with the cards on a deeper, personal level. You will want to use a tarot deck that you have worked with before. Take out the Fool card and study it. What emotions does the card evoke in you? What do you think of when you see the Fool? Don't worry about what the official meaning is, just think about your personal reaction to the card. Write this down.

Go through the rest of the major arcana and contemplate each card, writing down your thoughts and feelings about each. Note if cards seem to be connected, if certain cards turn you off, or if you are drawn to others. This gets you started looking at the tarot from a personal perspective, which you can then extend to the rest of the deck when minor arcana cards come up in readings.

Keep in mind that this is a personal interpretation of the tarot and so will be most relevant to your own personal readings. But the exercise will get you comfortable with going beyond the book definitions of the cards. This can be helpful if you end up doing a reading for another. It will also help train your mind to look beyond the obvious and tap into your intuition when you are in other situations.

A Witch Is Self-Aware

Knowing yourself is absolutely necessary for magic to work. This goes beyond knowing your astrological sign or favorite color. Knowing how you mentally process problems, what elements you align with, and what you can and cannot do physically all help you become a better witch. And that is the focus for this chapter.

Self-awareness comes in two forms: public and private. The public form is being aware of how you appear to others, whereas the private form is being aware of your internal state. The form I'm discussing here is private self-awareness. While it is good to know how the people around you see you, society puts too much emphasis on outward appearances. Being too tied up in people's perceptions of you can hinder your witchcraft, as you spend too much time focusing on what your practice looks like and not enough on what it means. Instead, I want to focus on the private, internal self-awareness and why that is important to your practice.

Improving your self-awareness has multiple benefits. First, by knowing yourself, you can create spells and rituals that better serve your intentions. You can choose spell components, types of spells, and more based on your own personal strengths. This gives your magic additional power and focus. Second, you gain more confidence. You can speak openly and easily about your needs and desires to the universe because you know what they are. This confidence will help you hone your intentions to a single point, and you won't be distracted by superfluous details. Finally, the knowledge that comes with self-awareness makes you secure in your values and morals. This will help you know when and how to act in a way that aligns with your core beliefs.

Your motivations, your strengths and weaknesses, your cultural background, and your family history all play a role in your witchcraft, whether you know it or not. By delving into these, you can better understand those things that might be unconsciously influencing you. Of all the lessons in *A Witch Is*, this may be the most painful. However, it is important to push past the awkwardness and discomfort to figure out what is going on behind the scenes, magically speaking.

Know Yourself Through Shadow Work

"Know thyself" is an ancient Greek proverb carved into the temple of Apollo in Delphi. It is both a command and a magic spell. Power resides in those two words, but most people are not willing to do the work to realize it. With how hectic day-to-day life is just to keep a roof over our heads and food in the pantry, there is often not any time for cultivating any meaningful sense of self-awareness. Additionally, today's society is antithetical to deep, meaningful introspection, unless it comes with a price tag attached to it. To truly know yourself requires you to carve out the time to do so. However, it doesn't cost a penny.

Shadow work is one exercise that can help you with your self-awareness. We discussed shadow work briefly in chapter 4, but here we're going to get into the nitty-gritty of it. The process is easy enough to explain, but engaging in it can be difficult and painful, especially if you haven't spent much time looking into yourself before now. If you have never done any kind of deep self-introspection before, you will want to be mentally and emotionally prepared. Make sure that you have plenty of time to do the work, without distractions, and make sure you have aftercare plans in place for when you are done.

To truly know yourself requires you to carve out the time to do so.

What Is Shadow Work?

Simply put, shadow work is the process by which one integrates their shadow self into their conscious mind. The term *shadow self* originated with the psychiatrist Carl Jung and refers to an unconscious self that is made up of desires, emotions, and impulses that are hidden from our conscious self. Despite being hidden, this shadow self influences us, often manifesting as anxiety or maladaptive behaviors that can affect our self-confidence, relationships, and other areas of our lives. Therefore, shadow work is an attempt to bring the shadow self to light and to work through the parts that negatively affect us.

The importance of shadow work in light of self-awareness is that it uncovers unconscious biases and motivations that could be affecting your magic and witchcraft. If you were part of a fundamentalist Christian religion, for example, you might find working with deities difficult because you have negative associations with god figures. Pushing yourself to have a relationship with these deities, then, might keep your magic from working because of that negativity. By addressing the root of the problem, you can get to a point where you are better able to interact with those deities.

Identifying Your Shadow Self

The first step in shadow work is to identify your shadow self. This tends to be the most painful part of the process as you are looking at parts of yourself that are less than ideal. This is digging down into the messy, swampy parts of yourself. Just as some people avoid looking in mirrors or having pictures of themselves taken because they don't like what they see, many will avoid looking inward because the picture might not be flattering. However, keep in mind that your shadow self is internal—no one can see it but you. And you can change it through the attention you give it.

Because we are witches, we are going to turn to our divination tool to identify our shadow self. Use the divination tool you are most familiar and comfortable with. You are going to ask it questions designed to bring your shadow self to the forefront. Ask the following questions of your oracle:

- What is the nature of my shadow self?
- What lessons can I learn from my shadow self?
- What ways can I integrate my shadow self?

Use these questions as springboards to follow-up questions: "What do I need to release? What do I need to forgive myself for? Where do I need to seek healing?" Record the answers you get in your book of shadows (if you keep one), your journal, or even the Notes app in your phone.

Next, you are going to use the answers to build a profile of your shadow self. Write down what they look like, what their main emotions are, and what lessons they are there to teach you. This is like building an image of your ideal self, but it is your subconscious self instead. You can draw or create a collage of this shadow self, if that is easier for you than writing it down.

Integrating Your Shadow Self

Identifying your shadow self is just the first step in shadow work. Now you get to engage in the equally messy part of integrating it into your conscious self. Typical activities for integration involve journaling, affirmations, and meditation. However, I suggest using your astral residence for this purpose. For this exercise, you'll need to have plenty of time without distractions. You'll also want to have your aftercare protocols in place (so have food ready if that is part of your aftercare, have your bath tools set up and ready to go if that is how you do aftercare, etc.).

Start by entering your astral residence however you usually do. Once there, take a moment or two to center and ground yourself. This can be a very emotional experience, and you want to be calm for the beginning of it. Next, visualize your shadow self. Use the profile you made earlier to help you in this part. Your shadow self might look like a version of you, but it also might look nothing like you at all. It may manifest as a swirl of energy, a particular smell, or even only as an emotional response. However you visualize it is valid.

Once it has manifested, look at your shadow self with love. Visualize pink light emanating from your heart and bathing the shadow self. Tell it, "I love you. I hear you. I am taking your lessons to heart." Continue to tell your shadow self words of affirmation. The point of this is to come to a place of acceptance of those parts of yourself that are hidden from your conscious mind. Thank your shadow self for the lessons it has to teach you, and give it forgiveness for those parts that negatively affect you. Tell it that you accept the good it has for you, while also gently rejecting those things that are damaging to your mental well-being.

After you have spent time at this, it is time to bring your shadow self into your conscious self. You can do this by simply visualizing the shadow self merging with your body. Feel it settle into your form as another part of you. The shadow self is not in control, but it is a part of you that provides its own kind of wisdom. Settle it into yourself and then thank it again for integrating with you. Sit with the feeling for a while just to get used to this new state of being.

This is an emotional process, and you might be moved to tears. You might feel anger, you might feel depressed, or you might feel giddy with happiness. Let yourself feel those emotions, knowing that you are in a safe space and that those feelings are valid. Once you feel ready, return to your physical body and engage in your self-care routine. You might want to journal on the shadow work you just underwent to fully process what happened. You may also need to repeat this activity more than once to fully integrate your shadow self. That is okay. Shadow work is a process that can last a lifetime, depending on how dedicated you are to the work.

Finding Your Personal Path

While our witchy ancestors were generalists, working magic with what they had on hand, modern witchcraft has come to recognize several different paths and practices. The different paths tend to focus on a specific type of magic based on the tools used or the elements the witch keys into when casting spells, or it can be arranged along cultural and geographical lines. There are kitchen witches, green witches, cottage witches, Appalachian witches, Welsh witches, Scandinavian witches, and more. There are even atheist and Christian witches. With so many different paths one can take, it can be overwhelming to know which one, if any, is right for you. This is where self-awareness comes in.

Finding what kind of magic works best for you involves some self-reflection on your part. This is the basis for all those "What kind of witch are you?" tests you can find online. There will be forms of magic that you are drawn to and types that you want nothing to do with. For example, I have no affinity with water magic. Having grown up in Wyoming, a landlocked state, I never got a feel for working with water. Similarly, I am not drawn to elemental magic. However, divination and sewing magic are both my jam.

To start deciding what kind of magic works for you, consider some of the following types of witchcraft:

- Scrying and divination
- Herbalism
- Elemental magic
- Spirit work
- Crystal magic
- Kitchen witchery
- Glamour magic
- Sigils
- Candle magic

This is not meant to be an exhaustive list, but it should give you a starting point. Note which of the above you are drawn to.

If none spark an interest, note which ones you definitely wouldn't enjoy and strike them off. You should have at least a couple that you find enjoyable. Focus on those types of magic. Research and experiment with them. If you don't get results, move on to another form. Don't be afraid to try new forms of magic until you find one that works for you.

The type of witch you call yourself can change over the years. I have gone from describing myself as an October witch (someone who only felt witchy in October) to a hedge witch to currently a witchcrafter. My title could change again as I age and find other labels that better fit how I feel about magic. Don't be afraid of that change. It doesn't make you an imposter or fake. It points to your continued evolution in your practice. You may also find a label that fits and that you never change. That's okay too. It shows that you have a good handle on who you are and what your path looks like.

You also don't have to label your path. Labels are helpful in guiding you to information that will be useful in your practice, but you shouldn't let them limit you. There is a reason that many witches call themselves "eclectic" in that they take what they need from different paths to suit their needs. As long as you aren't engaging in cultural appropriation or taking from closed practices, you are generally okay to follow a path that has no label.

Another way to narrow down what path best fits your personality and proclivities is to use the personal correspondences you came up with in the exercise "Creating Your Own Magical Correspondences" on page 55. You can also refer to the list of witchy qualities that you came up with in the exercise "Your Witchy Qualities" on page 75. Both of these lists offer insights into those things that fit your personal magical style. Look at the materia magica that you work with regularly. Do you prefer crystals or herbs? Perhaps you have an affinity for candle spells or divination. These preferences provide clues to what kind of magic you are best at.

Divination can be a useful tool in finding your path. A pendulum and pendulum board can give you yes-or-no answers to the question "Is this the path for me?" If you don't have a pendulum, it is easy enough to make one. Get a button, large charm, or heavy needle and thread it on a piece of thread that is about twenty inches long. You can even use a necklace in a pinch. For the board, take a piece of paper and draw an equilateral cross on it. Label the two ends of the vertical line "yes" and the two ends of the horizontal line "no." Mark the upper right-hand and lower left-hand corners as "unknown" and the upper left-hand and lower right-hand corners as "maybe."

To use the pendulum, hold it in your dominant hand with your hand about twelve inches above the board. With the pendulum dangling a few inches above the board, ask your yes-or-no questions. Concentrate on your question as the pendulum moves above the board and note which answer it swings toward. You can go through the list of possible paths you created to start narrowing the list down if it is long. Or you can focus on a specific path you are considering.

Once you have settled on a path, make use of it. Study up on the particulars of the practice. Find others who are on the same path and exchange information and ideas. Look for a community of like-minded witches either in real life or online. Even if you are an introvert, like I am, there is a benefit in finding others to share your successes and failures with. It might take time to find a group that you feel comfortable with. That is all part of the journey. And don't feel dissuaded if it takes time, or if you need to start your own community. As someone who works with Hestia, I know how hard it can be to find others who share the same path. The benefit of the internet, however, is that it is easier to connect with people once you find them.

Identifying Your Strengths and Weaknesses

As with other aspects of your life, you will have magical strengths and weaknesses. These present themselves as practices and kinds of magic you find easy or difficult to perform. Knowing where you excel and where you fail at magic is the point of self-awareness. It means that you can focus on magic that works for you. And it ensures that you don't waste your time on spells that won't work for you. It also gives you insight into areas that you can improve upon.

Weaknesses are often viewed as negative traits to have. However, I prefer to see them as guides to what better serves us. There is nothing worse than engaging in an activity that you don't enjoy and aren't skilled at because you feel like you have to do it a certain way. If you are casting a spell and resenting it the entire time you are working the spell, the magic will falter and fail. If we know our weaknesses, we can avoid that outcome. Then we can focus on what does. Remember, having a weakness is not a failing.

Engaging your intuition is a good way to start identifying your strengths and weaknesses. Your body can give you clues to what they are. Think of the last time you cast a spell. What parts of it made you feel good? What parts left you cold? These are signs of what you enjoyed doing and what you didn't, which can point to what you are good at and where you are lacking. This intuitive process can be applied to spells before you cast them as well. When you are putting together a spell or ritual, note how your body reacts to the different phases and components. Is there any part you look forward to doing? Any parts that you hesitate to do? Listen to your body and note any strong emotional reactions.

Another way to figure out your strengths and weaknesses is by looking at your personal magical path. If you are a kitchen witch, cooking, the elements of fire and water, herbs and spices, and working with deities who are associated with the culinary arts might be your strengths. On the flip side, you might find working with crystals, the elements of air and earth, sigils, and divination difficult. A crystal-using witch might find that she has a black thumb when it comes to plants. Or if you are used to working with elemental magic, you might find more physical aspects of magic hard to master.

You can also engage in deep self-reflection through practices like journaling, divination, and meditation. Work with journal prompts such as "What kinds of magic do I particularly enjoy?" and "Which ones do I find tedious?" Ask your preferred divination method what your strengths and weaknesses are. When it comes to meditation, use the following to help get in touch with your subconscious mind.

Reflect on your past experiences with spellcasting and magic. When was a time that a spell worked? When was a time that it didn't? Look at what you did, what the components were, and how you performed the spell to figure out what that means for your strengths and weaknesses. This is where writing down your spellwork and journaling before and after casting the spell come in handy. You can record not only what you did but how you felt while you were working the magic, which can give you clues to what you are good at, magically speaking, and where you are lacking.

Ultimately, this is an area where you have to be honest with yourself. That can be difficult at first, especially if you have never engaged in self-reflection before. It can also be hard if you are the type of person to think negatively about yourself. If this is the case, if you are one of those people who holds themselves to different standards than others, it might help to view yourself through a telescope rather than a microscope. By that, I mean looking at yourself from afar, as if you were viewing someone else, rather than scrutinizing every action, feeling, and thought. Taking a detached view of yourself can make it easier to identify both your strengths and weaknesses.

No matter how you go about it, you should be able to, by the end of this chapter, come up with at least a couple of ways in which you are magically strong and a couple in which you are magically weak. It is up to you to decide if you want to work on those weaknesses or just be aware of them. Some things might just not work for you, and that's okay. You shouldn't push yourself to cast spells in a way you have no affinity for. Focusing, instead, on your strengths means that you are setting yourself up for success in your practice.

Your Family and Cultural History of Witchcraft

There has been a movement over the last couple of decades against the prevalence of cultural appropriation in witchcraft. In the twentieth century, much of modern witchcraft was based on traditions and practices that belonged to marginalized groups. Practitioners would take bits and pieces of magic from wherever they wanted without considering what effect that would have on the cultures they were rifling through. However, this "eclectic" way of witchcraft has been slowly giving way to one that is less inclined to engage in such theft. The shift in attitude has been steady, if it has suffered from starts and stops at times. This, however, can leave a witch wondering where they should look for insight into the kind of witchcraft they should practice.

One answer to this question lies in the witch's cultural and family history, which brings with it a new set of challenges. You may not know where to start or who your family or culture is, or you might be estranged from them. All these problems can make researching your history painful. It is worth it to look into your familial history, however, if only to better understand where you come from. You may find that you don't want to engage in any of the cultural magic from certain sides of your family, and that information is just as useful to have as finding a magical tradition you can engage in.

When it comes to information from the internet, vet your sources.

If you know your cultural background, you have a place to start with identifying your historical magical practice. In recent years, there has been an explosion of books that dig into specific cultures and their magic. These books go beyond a generic "Celtic" banner and get into national and regional practices. The internet can provide even more resources for specific cultures. When it comes to information taken from the internet, you'll need to vet your sources, a topic that comes up in the next chapter on page 144.

Another place you can look for information is in the myths and legends of your culture. These will give you insights into the deities, archetypes, and heroes of the culture they belong to and can also provide clues to how magic was treated and used. If you can, find the stories in their original language, if you read it, or in highly rated translations. Collections of oral histories and stories are also useful for this purpose.

Family stories can offer a wealth of information as well, if you pay close attention. The little habits of various family members might have their origins in charms, superstitions, or other magics. Look into the religious practices of your family, as many Pagan beliefs and acts were subsumed by Christianity. Many different magical practices, such as Italian folk magic, are a mixture of Christianity and witchcraft.

What if you don't have any clues to your family or cultural history? What if you are adopted and know nothing about your birth family's history? Or what if you are estranged from your family and in such a way that attempting to reconnect with your culture is too painful at the moment? Or you can be like me, an American with such distant ties to other cultures that they are not relevant to my magical practice. I often joke that my family sprung up from beer nuts strewn across the Great Plains. But the reality, provided by my aunt's interest in our family's genealogy, is that we have ties to Scotland and Denmark. I could look into Scottish or Danish witchcraft, but because we are so far removed from our ancestors, I don't feel comfortable engaging in those traditions. My own magical practice is rooted in spirit work, candle magic with a dash of kitchen witchery, and working with Hestia.

You might find yourself in a similar situation. However, just because you might not feel a link to your ancestral origins, that doesn't mean there aren't cultural witchcraft practices that you can engage in. America has its own traditions: Southern American and Appalachian witchcraft, Irish American and Italian American folk magic, among others. America is full of various regional traditions, and if you look locally, into the region you are part of, you are more than likely to find one that fits you. There are also practices that aren't closed and that might resonate with you. Plenty are open to various practitioners and can provide a welcoming atmosphere to all comers.

The point of all this is not to reduce your experience and self-knowledge to one of simple genetics or family ties. Knowing your history and where you come from gives you keys to a part of you that it influences, even if unconsciously. Additionally, being able to figure out where you are from allows you to see where you are going more clearly. It allows you to identify any generational trauma that you might be carrying and begin the process of healing it. And, finally, it helps you tap into a well of magic that you might not have otherwise known was available to you.

Knowing your family and cultural background can also help you figure out what kind of path you should be following at this point in time. If you haven't identified a path using the methods in the "Finding Your Personal Path" section of this chapter (see page 118), that might be a sign that you should be focusing on a cultural take on witchcraft rather than a categorical path.

Self-awareness doesn't come easily to me. Having been raised to put others before myself, I feel selfish spending time thinking about myself. However, I quickly learned, as I advanced in my magical practice, that if I didn't look deeply into who I was and what I wanted, my witchcraft would suffer. Spending time figuring out what kind of magic works for you, where your strengths and weaknesses are, and doing shadow work will help you fine-tune your magic so that you see better results.

 EXERCISES 

The following exercises are meant to help you in your self-reflection. They dig into your conception of yourself as well as your ancestors. Take your time when you do these exercises, as they can dig up a lot of unpleasant emotions. Both of these exercises will benefit from you practicing grounding before you engage in them and self-care afterward.

Who Am I Collage

You'll need:

- Your book of shadows (if you keep one) or a sheet of paper
- Magazines to cut pictures from
- Stickers
- Stencils
- Markers
- Colored pencils
- Other art supplies
- Tape or glue

In this exercise, you are going to make a collage about yourself using the self-awareness information you learned from this chapter. If you want to go digital, use a photo or art program like Canva, or you can even create a Pinterest board with pins that represent who you are magically.

This is where you can get into the fine details of your self-awareness. Add your zodiac sign to your collage, your favorite color, your birthstone, your favorite crystal and herb. Add in the magical correspondences you came up with from the exercise "Creating Your Own Magical Correspondences" on page 55. Add in the list of witchy qualities you came up with in the exercise "Your Witchy Qualities" on page 75. Consider adding in items like the tarot card to which you feel the most connection. Include things like your rising sign, the element you are most attuned to, and your Myers–Briggs personality type.

Once you have completed your collage, keep it on your altar, if it isn't attached to a journal or book of shadows. If it is digital, you can save it as an image file and then set it as the background of your computer or laptop. You want the collage somewhere you can see it and reference it regularly. This way you can keep in the forefront of your mind just who you are as a witch. When you are curious about a new spell or materia magica or magic concept, you can go back to your collage and see how it aligns with who you are.

The collage is not a static item. You can add to, subtract from, or even remake it as you change and grow. It is meant to be a snapshot of your self-awareness at the present moment. And it provides a handy way to see how you have evolved and grown in your magic practice.

Ancestor Work

YOU'LL NEED:

- Photos of ancestors
- Small bowl or cup for offerings

- Frankincense incense
- Small candle
- Candleholder

Very few of us can pick up the phone and talk with a relative who is also a practicing witch. For the majority of us, we need to go back a bit further than our grandparents or great-grandparents to tap into ancestral magical wisdom. Fortunately, there are ways we can reach out to our ancestors to access information and support in our magical journey. For this exercise, you are going to set up an ancestral altar and invite your ancestors to come to you to share their wisdom.

To start, set out a small space where you can set up your altar. You don't need much room, and it doesn't even have to take up a horizontal space: you can create an altar solely made of a collection of photos and pictures hung on the wall.

Choose photos of your ancestors, if you have any. If not, choose photos or pictures of people who could be spiritual ancestors. These are individuals you don't have a direct blood relation to. Spiritual ancestors can be anyone, as long as there is some sort of tie that you can trace, even if it is just on a spiritual level. They also don't have to be "real" people to be ancestors: individuals from mythology, folk heroes, and people from stories can all serve as spiritual ancestors. Keep in mind to be respectful of these people if they are real. Take into consideration whether or not the person would welcome being your ancestor. Be cognizant of barriers such as racial tensions. For example, is it appropriate for a white woman to claim Tituba as a spiritual ancestor when she was an enslaved Native American? Be considerate when considering whom you want to claim as spiritual ancestors.

Set up the photos or pictures in the altar space. Light the incense and use it to cleanse the space. Put an offering in the bowl or cup. Water is a perfectly fine offering, as are coins (like pennies), honey, olive oil, and flowers. Light the candle and invite your ancestors to join you. Speak to them as you would if they were standing right in front of you. Ask to have a relationship with them and outline what you will do in return for their wisdom. This could be something as simple as continuing to leave offerings on the altar or a more complicated action like volunteering at a cultural center or museum. Once you have made your request and offer, be silent and let whoever has decided to show up speak to you. If no one does, snuff the candle and try again later. It may be that your ancestors will show up in other ways: via dreams or signs in the waking world.

You don't have to accept the help of whoever comes to you. If an ancestor you don't feel comfortable working with answers, you can politely thank them for the offer but decline. This is supposed to be a relationship that is beneficial to both parties, and it can't be if you don't like working with the other.

Return to your ancestor altar regularly. Make sure to fulfill whatever promises you've made to honor your ancestors in exchange for their information. Keep the altar dusted and clean, disposing of old offerings. Light the incense and candle whenever you are engaging with the altar, as that will signal to you and your ancestors that you want to talk. The more you work with them, the more readily they will manifest to offer insight, advice, and support.

A Witch Is Knowledgeable

Knowledge, they say, is power. And for a witch, this is especially true. We look to nature, to others, and even to ourselves for information that helps fuel our magic. The number of witchcraft books that are published each year is testament to the insatiable appetite that witches have for information.

Being knowledgeable is more than just knowing facts and figures. It includes being able to critically think about the information one comes across and then applying that knowledge. A witch will take every opportunity to find the lesson in every experience. They aren't afraid of differing viewpoints and opinions. And they can evaluate new information and decide if it fits with their personal beliefs or not.

Witches never stop learning. There is so much information out there that it is impossible to know it all. New information and ways of seeing are appearing every day. It can be overwhelming to think about everything we don't know. Additionally, it can be difficult to encounter new knowledge that invalidates what we thought we knew. If we keep an open and flexible mind, however, such changes shouldn't be intimidating. Approaching every day as an opportunity to learn something new gives us a plasticity of the mind that can make changes in long-held beliefs easier to accept.

This has never been truer than it is today. For example, I have written a book on the wheel of the year called *The Natural Home Wheel of the Year*. When I was researching and writing about it, I missed a lot of the discussion and criticism of the concept. Much of the wheel of the year was created by Gerald Gardner and Ross Nichols in the 1950s and 1960s, and later added to by Aidan Kelly. Much of the information on the history of the sabbats and the wheel of the year is appropriation of various Celtic and Welsh holidays, myths, and religions or complete fabrications. None of this information made it into my book, although I am aware of it now. Knowing that this is the case, however, I still find value in what I wrote, as the wheel of the year has become a major religious and cultural event for many Pagans. Learning about the discussion and criticism has instead given me deeper insight into the path I follow and has reminded me that I cannot take claims of "ancient Celtic beliefs and practices" at face value.

And this is what it means to be a witch, to keep an open and curious mind. If we become calcified in our thinking, refusing to incorporate new information into our lives, we'll end up missing out on a richer, more balanced practice. Easy answers and unchanging beliefs are not part of witchcraft.

Being a Problem-Solver

Having knowledge is the important first step to solving problems. If you don't understand the scope and nature of the obstacle you face, then how can you overcome it? When approaching a problem that you wish to solve with magic, you need to ask yourself not only what outcome you wish to achieve but also what the results will be. Journaling can help you with the first part of the equation. This allows you to explore different possibilities and decide which one would be the best outcome. You want to take into account not only yourself but also anyone else who might be affected by the problem, your magic, and the result. Remember to be specific, asking for the result you want in clear terms. Leaving things vague allows the universe and your magic to seek the most literal path of least resistance to fulfill your intentions. When it comes to figuring out what the results of your magic will be, that's when you turn to divination before you cast the spell. This sort of spell reconnaissance ensures that you will have the best results from your magic.

It is the knowledge you gain as you continue to learn in your practice that will be the best aid to problem-solving, however. Divination and journaling will only get you so far. You need a solid foundation of knowledge to fill in the gaps. Where you get this knowledge from can vary, depending on how you learn, and we'll cover different ways to learn later in the chapter. Just know now that the more you know, the better you will be able to overcome different problems.

The most relevant example of witchy problem-solving involves correspondences. As you've seen while working through *A Witch Is*, any object can have any number of magical correspondences. These energies and powers can overlap with other materia magica so that you have a variety to choose from depending on availability, budget, and personal preference. This means that when you are following a spell that asks for patchouli essential oil and you don't have that on hand, you can look into substitutes. For this example, let's imagine that the spell is for creating an ancestor veneration oil. Patchouli is used in summoning spirits, so you start looking at other plants and oils that can be used as a substitute and find that dandelion leaf, mint, catnip, and rosehips can all be used to call in spirits. At this point, you could substitute the patchouli oil with mint essential oil or make an anointing oil from olive oil and the other herbs.

Let's take this type of problem-solving even further. Say you are trying to work out the right timing for a spell. You want to cast a spell during the full moon; however, life is getting in the way of you being able to schedule time to do the spell at that time. You can turn to the weekly or hourly planetary alignments to attempt the spell on a Monday or during the hours associated with the moon to tap into that luscious lunar energy. All it takes is thinking outside the box to come up with solutions to whatever obstacles you face magically.

The point of these two examples is to show that you do not have to know everything all at once. It is okay to be unsure of how to proceed, as long as you are willing to do the research to figure out what you need to do. Google, Pinterest, and social media sites grant us access to a wealth of information. There are books on every conceivable topic out there that can be consulted. All you need to do is take the time to look up whatever you are interested in and then apply what you have learned to overcome whatever obstacle you are facing. You will, of course, need to vet your sources, and we get into that later in the chapter. But for now, I only want you to get comfortable with the idea that research is a necessary part of witchcraft.

You do not have to know everything all at once.

The final aspect of problem-solving for the witch is knowing what kind of magic is suitable for the problem at hand. There are so many different types of spells and spellcasting, which gives the witch a great deal of flexibility when dealing with problems. Deciding what kind of spell to use depends on what kind of magic you are most attuned to, what you have on hand, and what kind of solution you are looking for. Long-term results, or those problems that will take time to rectify, benefit more from spells that have physical components you can refer to over time. This includes enchanting items to keep on hand, such as spell pouches, talismans, and spell jars. If it is a problem that needs a quick solution, or if you don't want to leave evidence of the spell behind, you can use candle spells, chants, or spells with components you discard after the spell has been cast. A quick guideline is to use the element of earth for anything that needs to stick around, water for anything that needs to flow or have movement, fire for anything that needs to be transformed, and air for anything nonphysical.

Cultivate Relationships

Community is an important part of witchcraft. I say this as a witch who is an introvert and often finds the outside a bit too "peopley" most of the time. However, even though I would rather be sitting at home with my books and my sewing machine, I still recognize that relationships are necessary if one is going to work magic. Not only does the witch gain access to the information and knowledge of others in the community, but they can gain mutual support.

Seeking out other, like-minded people, mentors, and even mentees helps you exchange ideas and share knowledge. This can take the form of something as formal as a coven or as casual as meeting for coffee once a month. You don't have to engage in a community in person, either. There are plenty of digital ways to connect with other witches. The point is to find a place where you can engage with other witches.

These communities give you others whom you can bounce ideas off of and go to for advice. But you should not just be there for your own benefit. You should be giving back as much as you take from the community, providing your own insight and knowledge in a mutual exchange. This back-and-forth helps strengthen the bonds of the community, which can come in handy later if group spellwork is ever required. That kind of work necessitates a level of trust that can only be built over time and with great care.

Be aware that there can be harmful communities out there. Gatekeeping, toxic positivity, spiritual bypassing, and other forms of unhealthy behaviors can pop up in even the best communities. If you aren't one of the moderators or organizers of the community, there might be little you can do to deal with those members who bring it down. However, that doesn't mean you can't stand up for what you believe in. All members of a community are obligated to help maintain its health. To that end, don't be afraid to call out problematic behavior when you see it. For every person who pushes back to maintain the integrity of a space, there are many others who will support them but didn't feel able to do so on their own. Should the space become overwhelmingly toxic, you can leave. Don't feel like you have to stick around a community that has become a detriment to your mental and magical health.

Community support doesn't have to only consist of humans, either. There are spirits, deities, ancestors, and others you can reach out to in order to create a relationship. Those spirits that are connected to the land you are on are some of the most powerful ones you can work with, as you both have a mutual interest. Take time to learn about the genii loci that are part of where you live. Introduce yourself and let them know that you are open to any wisdom they may be willing to share with you. Find out if they require offerings or gifts of service in return and work out what that would look like. And then: listen. Let the spirits speak to you about what they want to tell you. It might not seem to have anything to do with what you want to know. The spirit may simply wish to tell you something that is important to it. That's okay. If you are puzzled about something the spirit has told you, you can engage in divination to work out its meaning.

The spirits you work with aren't limited to genii loci. There are plant and crystal spirits that you can create a relationship with as well. This kind of relationship develops over time, as you find yourself working with the same materia magica over and over. You'll find that you resonate with certain plants and crystals. When you have identified such potential allies, you can use meditation to reach out to their spirits and see about establishing a relationship with them. Not only will this give you another source of magical information, but you will find that your spellwork is more effective because the spirit of the materia magica is working with you to achieve your goals.

One of the benefits of a community is mutual support. The support one gains from a community is especially important during a time when people can still be threatened with arrest over practicing their craft. In times when there is a rise of Christian nationalism in the United States, as well as far-right movements in other countries, it is vital that witches stick together.[15] A solitary witch is easier to target than several standing strong together. Mutual support can range from offering funds to help witches in

15. For example, white supremacist Nick Fuentes has said that "these people… that are communing with demons and engaging in this sort of witchcraft and stuff, and these people that suppressing the name Christ and suppressing Christianity, they must be absolutely annihilated." "White Christian Nationalist Calls for Death Penalty for All Non-Christians," Freedom from Religion Foundation, December 14, 2023, https://ffrf.org/news/releases/white-christian-nationalist-calls-for-death-penalty-for-all-non-christians/.

need to casting spells to aid them. As with all things magical, you want to make sure that you are being specific and focused with your spellwork.

Spell for Finding a Community

If you are still working to find a community that best suits your needs, try this spell.

You'll need:

- Slips of paper and a writing utensil
- Sage incense
- Jar
- Three bay leaves
- Fennel seeds
- Thyme leaves
- Blue chime candle

Take the slips of paper and write down what you are looking for in a community. Also write down what you bring to the community. Remember, this is a two-way street and you want to give back what you get out of a space.

Using the sage incense, cleanse the jar inside and out. Add the slips of paper to the jar. Next, add the bay leaves, fennel seeds, and thyme to the jar. Seal the jar and place a blue candle on the lid. Light the candle and say an affirmation like "I find comfort, support, and knowledge in community." Let the candle burn down to seal the jar.

Place the jar where you will see it often. Once a day, give the jar a shake while focusing on the community you wish to join. Make sure to go about doing the mundane work to support your spell-casting: join a local witchy group, find places online where you can engage in magical dialogue, or start a community of your own. And when you have found the place for you, open the jar. Burn the slips of paper and dispose of the herbs by burying them.

Ways to Learn

Our society today places a lot of emphasis on authoritative learning: that is, learning in an environment where students are taught by an authority (i.e., a teacher). Knowledge, we are taught, needs to be passed from someone with greater knowledge to those with less knowledge. And, in many specific applications, this is the only way teaching works. Structured classes are helpful for children who need to be monitored and guided on the path of learning. However, as one gets older, this type of learning can be less helpful. When we invest all the power into "experts," we diminish our own knowledge and capabilities. And so, for the witch, it is important to know there are other ways to learn. And the witch will direct their own education via reading, going out into nature, talking with spirits, and listening to their intuition.

As an author, I am always going to point to the vast amount of information that can be accessed via books, blog posts, and articles. I've mentioned before that whatever you wish to learn, there is probably a book about it. Social media provides other sources of information, often in bite-size chunks, that can help introduce you to concepts and techniques. For those for whom reading isn't a strong suit, there are videos and podcasts. These also cover a broad range of topics. And there are always audiobooks. With so many different media forms out there, witches have no end of choice in how they can continue to learn.

Reading books and listening to podcasts is still a form of authoritative learning, however. Authors, influencers, and podcasters are given a certain amount of authority by the fact that they are published or are making the media others consume. This is not to say the information they provide isn't valuable, but there are other ways for a witch to learn that aren't based on authority. One of those ways is to turn to nature.

Nature, a Witch's First Teacher

Going out into nature provides an education that can't be found in other people's experiences. This is where you must rely on your abilities to listen and to reason to put together the lessons that nature gives you. By careful observation and opening yourself up to messages that come not via the spoken or written word, you can tap into magical knowledge that is meant solely for you and your practice.

Witchcraft is rooted in nature. The elements, herbs and plants, stones, and water of the earth are all fuel for magic. Much of magic is tied to the passage of seasons, the phases of the moon, and the path of the sun as it passes through the sky above. Sacred springs provide access to various energies that can be harnessed for magical purposes. Animals carry messages from spirits and deities to us. All of this acts as a living grimoire for the witch who knows how to listen and learn.

As a witch, you should familiarize yourself with the land you live on. This includes its past, who lived there before, and what spirits reside there now. You can create a relationship with a piece of land by providing care for it, picking up trash, tending to the plants, and the like. And in return, you can ground yourself, meditate, and listen to the land for whatever wisdom it is willing to provide. Start in your own backyard, if you have one, or in a local park. Learn about the plants growing there, what kind of soil makes up the earth, what animals live in the area. Look for the magical correspondences of the plants and animals. Meditate in the space and see if there are any genii loci living there.

Once you have familiarized yourself with the space, practice little magics in it. Make offerings of water or energy to the trees and plants. Cast a protective circle around the space against littering and vandalism. Ask permission of the land for materia magica and start including the local plants, earth, and water in your spellcasting at home. Tapping into local energies will give your spells greater power as the connection between you and the land is closer and stronger.

Unverified Personal Gnosis

Your own personal experience, or unverified personal gnosis, is just as important a path to knowledge as any other. Don't be put off by the "unverified" part of this. All that means is that you have information that hasn't been verified by anyone else. Those beliefs and understandings that you come by via your own experience are valid for you, as long as they aren't harmful to others. Racist, sexist, and bigoted beliefs are limiting and are just as harmful to you as to others. When you come across something that you believe to be true, ask yourself if it is kind. The answer to that question will tell you if it is a belief that you should be incorporating into your life. If it is kind, then it is worth pursuing to assess if it is true for you. If it isn't kind, then you can discard it and move on.

You can also go to your community with your belief to discuss it with others. This allows you the opportunity to stress test it and your reasonings. Others may have the same beliefs as you do, and then you have more information to support what you believe and why you believe it. It may be that others haven't ever thought of things in this way, and they may not agree with your conclusions. Then, through the process of discussion, you can either strengthen your reasoning or abandon the belief. Either way, you have learned something.

Let's say that you have been working with a particular plant ally, say catnip. This plant is usually associated with the Egyptian goddess Bast. But perhaps in your work with catnip it has informed you that it is also associated with the Norse goddess Freya. This is because she has a chariot that is drawn by cats. You might then use it as a springboard for working with Freya or with the cats who pull her chariot. Or it might lead you to using catnip in spells to deal with protection, warfare, and conflict, in the way that a cat engages its claws in fights. This is a connection that other witches might not make and might even argue against. This knowledge doesn't harm anyone. And so this might be a bit of personal information that is meant solely for your own benefit.

Vet Your Sources

There is a vast amount of information out there, especially when it comes to witchcraft. The practice has been around for literal millennia, meaning one can feel overwhelmed when trying to learn. This is where it is important to engage critically with your sources. Accepting everything that is provided at face value can lead to confusion or conflict with your core beliefs. Vetting your sources can be difficult when it comes to witchcraft and magic, however, as much of it is based on unverified personal gnosis. In that case, we have to rely on other ways to evaluate information we come across. This involves making use of our intuition and having a firm understanding of our values. The two need to be used together, along with looking at general consensus and an understanding that there may be cultural differences that account for conflicting information.

We start with that last point. Different cultures will have different approaches to magic. Some cultures engage in ritual animal sacrifice, a practice that those outside of the culture might find distressing. Other paths might make use of bones, fur, and skins in their practice, whereas others would not use animal parts. In a less visceral example, Eastern practices have different directional correspondences from Western practices. Other cultures may also have assigned different correspondences for various herbs, crystals, animals, and deities. And this is not even taking into account the fact that most magical correspondences written for plants are based on Western European perspectives and tend to ignore plants from Asia, Africa, and the Americas.

Knowing what your values and beliefs are will help with this. Practices that go against your beliefs are then not ones you want to engage in. If you believe in the threefold law, for example, you may be opposed to hexing. It is a good idea to have at least a nominal understanding of what your ethics and beliefs are before you embark on your path, but you can also clarify those beliefs as you learn about magic. When you come across new information, compare it to your morals. Is it in alignment with them, or is it in opposition to them? Would engaging in a particular practice put you at odds with your beliefs? If so, that practice may not be for you. Knowing what you believe in gives you a criterion for new magical information.

Your intuition can also help you decide what makes sense for you. When you are reading a book, watching a video, or listening to a podcast on witchcraft, tune in to your body. How does it feel when you consider what you are reading or hearing? Is there tension in your body? Does your stomach clench or your chest tighten? That is a sign your intuition is rejecting what you are learning. If instead you have a feeling of "rightness" or lightness or your body is relaxed, then that is a sign of your intuition accepting the information.

Of course, general consensus can come into play when vetting sources. There are certain aspects of witchcraft that have become standard over time. The role intention plays in magic, for example, or the correspondences for deities, herbs, and crystals. This is knowledge that started off as personal observations and that made sense to others. That's not to say that there aren't people who disagree with the common correspondences. That doesn't make those people wrong; it just means they have a different personal connection to those items. But the general consensus can give you a starting point, and if you come across information that goes against the grain, it behooves you to question why that is. You may come to decide the accepted meaning of a correspondence makes sense to you, or you may learn something new that fits better with your personal brand of witchcraft.

Take the time to compare various retellings and sources.

When it comes to myths, legends, and other material that is in the literary record, take the time to compare various retellings and sources. Read the original literature, if you can, or get a reputable translation. Myths, especially, have had various retellings and reinterpretations over the years, and so it benefits you to know the differences between them. Attempt to trace any information to the source, so that you know that what someone claims the myth, legend, hymn, or poem says is accurate. When an author makes a claim about something, check to see if they include footnotes or endnotes with sources.

Looking for sources on websites is just as important. It is so easy to copy and paste text that misleading or erroneous information can be spread far and wide. And with the rise of AI-generated texts, the chance of encountering false information is on the rise. Take any claims made on a website with a large grain of salt and attempt to track down where that information is coming from. You can do a web search for the exact phrasing to see if it is repeated on other websites or to try and track down where the claim originated.

Finally, consider the source of the material you are vetting. With the rise of self-publication, the ease with which one can post videos and writings to the internet, and the prevalence of social media, everyone and anyone can publish their own magical hot takes. I personally believe that this is a good thing, as it makes information more accessible. However, it does require that people exercise their critical thinking. Look at authors and their other posts, videos, and podcasts. Is their body of work in keeping with your stances on witchcraft and magic? Do they engage in cultural appropriation or problematic behavior? Are they sharing unique perspectives or just regurgitating what others have previously published? This is especially important to do when it comes to older books that may have approaches and attitudes that are outdated or even harmful. You might even decide to stick with traditionally published books, which have gone through an editorial process.

Learning about witchcraft isn't all about finding what is compatible with your personal beliefs, however. Do not be afraid to explore topics and viewpoints that you don't agree with. Being exposed to opinions that are in conflict with your own gives you a chance to reevaluate your position. Either you will discard thinking that no longer holds up or you will be reaffirmed in your position.

~~~

There is a world of magical knowledge out there just waiting to be discovered, and more information comes out each and every day. That can be overwhelming to even seasoned witches, especially when new information contradicts what has come before. But, as a witch, you owe it to yourself to seek out new knowledge. You also need to be constantly subjecting your beliefs to stress tests to make sure that they are still serving you. Being knowledgeable about witchcraft means that you are willing to drop information that is outdated. It can be daunting, knowing that what you might take as fact today could be disproven tomorrow. But that knowledge can also be exhilarating as you approach your witchcraft like a scientist, always poking and prodding your magic to find better, more effective techniques. Don't let the idea that a witch is knowledgeable overwhelm you. You can start small, learning one new thing a day.

 EXERCISES 

Even if you take a course on magic, learning is completely up to you. Witches tend to be self-motivated when it comes to gaining magical knowledge. And so the following exercises can get you started on putting your knowledge to practice and getting comfortable with doing magical research.
~~~

Third Visit to the Magical Pantry

You'll need:

- Your lists from "The Magical Kitchen Cupboard" (page 23) and "Back to the Magical Pantry" (page 57)
- Your cookbooks

We return once again to your pantry for this exercise. You identified the correspondences for each spice and herb in there in "The Magical Kitchen Cupboard" on page 23, and you came up with substitutions for them in "Back to the Magical Pantry" on page 57. Now it is time to put that knowledge in a place where you can consult it on a regular basis.

Pull down your recipe books. Turn to recipes that you make often. Next to the ingredients, write the properties that correspond to them. This way, when you next make the recipe, you will have the correspondences right at your fingertips. If you don't have favorite recipes, or if there are too many, copy your list of correspondences into the front of the recipe book so that they'll be there when you need them. For those who don't have a recipe book, post the list inside the pantry, near the spices.

The point of this exercise is to take the knowledge you've built and place it where you will have access to it. Information that stays locked inside a book of shadows or a computer file will do you no good. Being a witch is more than just collecting knowledge: it is putting that information to work.

Magical Research

As I've already mentioned in this chapter, a witch is always learning. In this exercise, you are going to use the vast resources available to you to research a topic that interests you. This can be something as broad as crystals or as specific as how to write a sigil. It should be a topic that you don't know much about.

Once you have chosen your topic, you are going to start your research. You must find three articles, three videos, and one book about your topic. The articles can be blog posts, social media posts, or articles in magazines or journals. The videos can be either social media short videos or longer-form ones. For the book, look up titles that cover the topic. Make use of online reviews to vet the book.

After you have located your sources, read and watch them. Then take some time to consider what the information they provide. Does what you read or watched make sense to you? Is it new information or something you already knew? How is the information presented, and do the authors seem credible? How does the information between the various sources compare and contrast? What does your intuition say about what you have learned?

Once you have gotten into the habit of using your critical thinking when consuming witchy media, you'll find that you can better weigh information for what makes sense for you.

A Witch Is Purposeful

With very few exceptions, witchcraft is deliberate. The more you practice it, the easier it will come to you, and you'll be able to apply it to any situation. But before you reach that point, you need to be purposeful in your witchcraft. This doesn't apply to only your magic but also your approach to your life as a witch. It covers the exciting part of magic, casting spells, but also the boring parts, like labeling your spell components in jars, boxes, and bags so you know what you have on hand.

The focus of this chapter is on how to gain greater success in your spellcasting through acting deliberately and purposefully. We return to the steps in "Creating Your Own Spells and Rituals" on page 42. They boil down to:

1. Identify the problem to be solved.
2. Decide your desired goal or outcome.
3. Figure out the best kind of magic to achieve your goal.
4. Gather the materials and decide the timing.

5. Cast the spell.
6. Use mundane actions to support your magic.

If you do the above, you are 90 percent there for a successful spell. But if you want to increase your odds of success, add two actions: setting SMART goals and divining before you cast your spell.

Being purposeful is not only about how you approach your magic but also about how you find meaning in it. Knowing why you believe and act the way you do is part of living purposefully, and that can be just as important for your practice as for your mundane life. If you can figure out what it is that you truly want to get out of your magic, you can close the gap between those two aspects of your life. This then leads to living a more magical life, one that is aligned with your practices and ethics and one in which you can thrive as a witch.

Goal-Oriented Magic

While magic is not possible without intent, results can vary based on many factors. One way to ensure a successful outcome is to focus on your desired goal. To increase your odds of success, use SMART goals. SMART is an acronym that stands for specific, measurable, achievable, relevant, and time-bound. It is a concept introduced by George T. Dolan in 1981, and though the concept was originally meant for business applications, it can be used in spellcasting.[16] Apply the parameters of SMART goals to your mag-

16. George T. Doran, "There's a S.M.A.R.T. Way to Write Management's Goals and Objectives," *Management Review* 70, no. 11 (1981): 35–36, https://community.mis.temple.edu/mis0855002fall2015/files/2015/10/S.M.A.R.T-Way-Management-Review.pdf.

ical objective before you cast your spell, and you'll find that your magic sees better and more consistent results.

Let's say you are in need of money. That is the problem. Now you need to focus on your goal. We'll go through all parts of the acronym using this example to give you an idea of how to write your SMART goals.

The first part, "specific," is the most important part of the acronym. You want to be certain that you have a clear goal in mind. This means being as detailed as possible when it comes to envisioning your desired outcome. Using our example—you need money—we can come up with various different ways to solve your problem. You could win the lottery. You could come into an inheritance. You could find some cash on the street. Or you could get a better-paying job. These are all different goals, and depending on your circumstances, each one might be possible (see "achievable" on the next page). If you choose to go the lottery route, you want to be very specific: Which lottery are you going to win? Perhaps you are looking for some extra cash to come your way: How much do you need, and will it come to you out of the blue or due to your own efforts? Maybe you decide that getting a better-paying job is the right choice. What kind of job are you thinking of getting? With what company? How much better paying will it be? This, again, is where brainstorming and journaling come in handy, as you can imagine what each possible goal would look like if it happened.

Next, you want to have a goal that is "measurable." It's hard to decide that you have succeeded if you don't have an idea of what success looks like to begin with. This aspect of the goal is anything you can measure. This can be as simple as whether you are better off once the goal is achieved than you are now. In the case of our example, perhaps you have a specific amount of money in mind.

Place that amount in your goal. There's a tendency to leave our goals vague and let the universe sort it out. But this is just a recipe for the magic to give you the bare minimum you ask for. Magic follows the path of least resistance, and if you only go with casting a spell for money, you could end up with getting a settlement check for seventeen cents in the mail. Don't be afraid to ask for exactly what you need when setting your goals.

Next, we move on to "achievable." This is the part of the acronym that can be the hardest for magic workers to settle on. Magic, after all, should make all things achievable, right? Well, yes, but as with everything, the details are in the fine print. Keep in mind, too, that achievable in many cases means "realistic." You are not going to learn to fly without an airplane or become invisible with magic. Returning to our example, say you decide to try for a new, better-paying job. Maybe the jobs you are looking at are all located out of the town or city where you currently live. Will you actually be able to move to take the position if offered it? Or maybe it requires you to have certain certifications or education to qualify. Will you be able to get those in time? If you chose the lottery as your ticket to wealth, are you actually buying tickets? What mundane actions are you able to take to support your magical work? If there are conditions or obstacles that will keep you from obtaining your goals, you need to take them into consideration as well. You might need to put your larger goal on hold to focus on these other issues first.

Don't be afraid to ask for exactly what you need when setting goals.

Goals should also be "relevant" to your problem. If you are facing eviction because of a shortfall of cash, some of the magical goals you've been looking at might not really be a good idea. You need to focus on goals that will solve the problem you are facing, as it is right now, instead of the problem that you think you have. In the case of the shortfall, you can't wait for a new job to start paying a higher wage—you need to act now. So a goal of reaching a certain amount in aid from friends and family might make more sense. Again, magic, like water, will seek out the lowest level in the most efficient way. When you structure your goals to be germane to the problem, you are providing it a path to follow instead of flinging your spell out into the aether and hoping for the best.

Finally, you want your goal to be "time-bound." Like with the measurable part of the SMART equation, this can trip witches up. We again don't want to put too many constraints on the magic, afraid that it will limit our results. However, think of your goals as guide rails for the magic. Instead of throttling it, the goals give it a target that is unmissable because it is so specific. Be concise and realistic when you set your deadlines. You want to give your magic time to work. If you need money soon, inform your magic of the date you need it by, rather than just leaving it open-ended. If you aren't comfortable with a concrete date, use timing such as "a year and a day" or "by the next full moon." Whatever deadline you choose, mark that day on your calendar and then let the magic do its work. When the date comes, use divination to find out why it didn't work, if it didn't. An example of a SMART goal for this situation would look like this: "I will bring in five hundred dollars by the end of the month through signing freelance contracts with two clients." This is a specific, measurable, achievable (presuming you are a freelancer), relevant, and time-bound goal. You know what it is that you are going to do, how you are going to do it, and when you are going to do it by.

Creating SMART goals will help you have a finely detailed, fully fleshed-out goal in mind when you start your spell. While it takes a little bit longer to make your goal via this method, the benefits are clear. Once you have practiced at it, the process will only take a few minutes.

Pre-Spellcasting Rituals

Before you actually cast your spell, there are actions you can take to set yourself up for success. The first is to spend some time divining to discover what the outcome of your spell will be. Another is to make sure that you have set the stage for the spellwork, checking that you have cleansed and created a safe environment in which to work your magic. And finally, you can ground and center to put yourself in the right frame of mind for your spellcasting.

Divination for Spellwork

I recommend divining before you cast spells, unless it is a quick one that you've had success with before. Divining before casting your spell can save you an immense amount of effort down the road. You can ask questions like "Will this spell work?" after you have gone through the process of creating your spell, but this is an inefficient way to go about it. Instead, it is better to consult your oracle after you have set your goal but before you have started figuring out what kind of magic to cast. It is also better to ask more open-ended questions. This is because they allow the universe to give you additional information. Yes-or-no questions don't allow for such insight.

Before you begin with your divination, sit quietly and focus on both the problem you are facing and your desired goal. You want to have both firmly in mind before you ask your questions. Once you are ready, ask the following questions as you draw your cards (or runes) or before you cast your charms or scry:

1. What advice can you give me on this spell?
2. What is working against my spell's success?
3. What is working toward my spell's success?
4. What will be my spell's outcome?

Asking first for advice gives the universe the opportunity to let you in on any blind spots you might have with regard to the problem, your goal, or the spell itself. It is often what we don't see that has the greatest impact on our actions. Knowing what is working against you can help you identify if there are factors in play, and the same is true for knowing what is working to your benefit. The answer to that question might uncover surprising allies in the situation. Finally, asking what the outcome of the spell will be lets you know if your goal will be achieved.

If the results of your divination are positive, you can then move on to the next step of deciding what kind of magic you should use to achieve your goals. If the results are negative, however, that points to something being wrong with either your perception of the problem or your stated goals. Further divination in the form of follow-up questions, such as "What can I do differently to achieve success?" can be asked for further insight.

Setting the Stage

When you are working magic, you want to start off in an environment that is conducive to spellcasting. While I don't want anyone to mistake aesthetic for utility, there are times when having "witchy" items around you helps create a mood you can then use to drive your intention and magic. If nothing else, having an action that you do for every spell and ritual to signal to your brain that it's time for magic will help you shift into the right frame of mind. This can be as elaborate as taking a cleansing bath, dressing in ritual clothing, lighting candles, playing music, and then casting a full circle around your workspace. Or it can be as simple as lighting a cone of incense and taking a moment to ground yourself. The point is to be consistent about what you are doing so that you set up a trigger to recognize when you are working magic versus taking mundane actions.

Of course, you don't have to engage in highly elaborate rituals to set up for working magic. At the minimum, just cleansing yourself and your space before you start is enough. You want to ensure that there are no stray or negative energies that can interfere with your magic. This is especially important if you are going to be using materia magica that you got from a store. You want to give it a quick smoke or sound cleansing. This is the equivalent of washing fruits and vegetables before you eat them. Cleansing yourself does the same, by ensuring you aren't bringing in any unhelpful energies.

Grounding and Centering

Finally, you want to make sure that you are in the right mind frame to work the magic. This means grounding and centering so that you can focus on your intent. With practice, the two actions can take as little as thirty seconds.

After cleansing yourself and your space, take the time to exchange any internal, unhelpful energies such as doubt, fear, and anxiety with the earth for calming, confident, and compassionate ones. Visualize the energies you want to get rid of as dark, black-blue smoke that goes through your grounding roots into the earth. Then draw up white energy to replace what you just got rid of.

Once you have grounded yourself, center by visualizing the white energy you've pulled up coming to rest at your center, either your solar plexus or your heart. Visualize and feel that energy dispersing through your body to fill every fiber of it. Feel a sense of calm spread throughout your limbs to your fingers and toes. You might feel a slight tingling sensation in your palms or at the back of your neck, but you should mostly just feel relaxed.

This state of body and mind will help you better focus on your intent as you work your spell. Engaging in any one of these pre-spellcasting rituals will ensure that you are casting a spell that will actually solve the problem you are facing. Doing all three together will increase your chances of success.

The Ritual and the Witch

When one gets down to it, ritual is just routine with meaning. The little acts you do throughout the day can be elevated to ritual just by putting a little significance into them. This is the magic behind stirring your coffee clockwise to bring blessings into your life, or when you say affirmations into the mirror as you go about your nightly skincare routine. This elevation of mundane tasks into something magical needs only your attention and your intention.

Rituals best serve daily needs, such as safety, happiness, and prosperity, rather than one-time needs like we discussed in the "Goal-Orientated Magic" section earlier. Rituals are also repeated on a timely basis rather than cast like spells. I always recommend that witches look at what they already do day to day to see if there is anything they can turn into a ritual. The benefits of this over creating a new ritual is that if it is something you do routinely, you are more likely to keep up with it over the weeks, months, and years.

Sit down with your book of shadows, if you have one, your journal, or even the Notes app on your phone and think about what you do on a daily or weekly basis. Maybe you go to the gym three times a week. Or maybe you take a walk in a nearby park each day during your lunch hour. Write down all the regularly scheduled activities you engage in. Don't ignore the smallest chore: making your bed, washing your face, getting dressed. Anything you do consciously and regularly can be turned into a ritual, no matter how small or insignificant you think it is.

Think about how you could turn your regular activities into a ritual. The workout example could be used for affirmations or even to cast a spell for continued good health. Your lunchtime walk could be turned into a walking meditation in which you commune with nature. Even the most mundane of tasks, such as washing the dishes or sweeping the floor, can be turned into an opportunity to cleanse and bring in blessings. The key is to have a magical mindset when you approach these different activities. Note next to each task you wrote down a way you could make it a ritual.

Thinking and writing it all down is just the first step, however. Now you need to implement the rituals. This might take time for you to do. If you forget or you are rushed and don't feel you have time, that's okay. Because it is a daily or weekly event, you will have an opportunity to engage in your ritual the next time. As long as you make a good faith effort to engage in the ritual you created, it will, over time, become second nature to you.

You don't have to focus on things you are already doing, of course. All rituals are made up, and there's nothing stopping you from creating one from scratch. The process is the same as turning an everyday task into a ritual, with the added step of first coming up with what that task will be. You can start with something that doesn't happen every day but weekly or monthly. For example, consider making a full moon ritual. This can involve moon gazing, setting out your crystals and tarot cards to charge under the full moon, making moon water, or casting a spell for prosperity. Keeping the ritual simple will make it more likely that you will do it.

When creating rituals, think about what you would like them to look, smell, sound, taste, and feel like. How often would you like to engage in them? What are you seeking to accomplish and get out of them? Answering these questions will help you build a ritual that has meaning for you. Also, consider creating rituals that you will enjoy. While giving magical meaning to unpleasant mundane tasks can help you engage in them, so too should you have some rituals that just make you happy. Life isn't meant to be toil and bother. It is meant to be enjoyed and celebrated.

It might be helpful to make use of calendars and phone alerts to schedule your ritual and set reminders. It might feel weird to do so at first, especially if you are a solitary practitioner, but doing so will help you build a strong foundation for your rituals. Over time, you'll become sure in your practice and won't need a calendar alert or have to refer back to your notes. For example, if you have decided to have a full moon ritual every month, put it on your calendar and set a reminder for the day before the full moon so that you aren't caught unawares. You don't have to keep the alarms forever. After a while, you will find that you don't need them to remind you of what you intend to do.

Life is meant to be enjoyed and celebrated.

Rituals can be hourly, daily, weekly, monthly, or even yearly. Don't overwhelm yourself with too many rituals. Unless you have no other obligations, like work, family, or friends, you could end up with more rituals than time. They then begin to feel like obligations and chores more than acts of connection. Stick with just a few to start. As you get more used to turning your regular activities into rituals, you'll find that you naturally continue to do so with everything you do. This is one of the keys to living a magical life, something we'll discuss in the next section.

Putting the Purpose in Your Practice

Being deliberate in your practice isn't the only way a witch is purposeful. There is also the question of finding the magic in everyday life, no matter how mundane. We witches have a different way of seeing when it comes to the world around us, and we can apply that special sight to all aspects of our lives, not just to those that are part of our practice. There are many different ways to create purpose in your path. We'll be focusing on three here: mindfulness, gratitude, and building relationships.

Mindfulness

Mindfulness might be the most difficult part of living purposefully. It requires a level of awareness that we often don't engage in due to the stressors of modern life. With so many different choices we have to make every day and the busyness of life, we often suffer from decision fatigue that leads to our brains shutting down and acting on autopilot. That mental shutdown keeps us from being aware of our inner thoughts and feelings and outer landscape.

The solution is to practice mindfulness and to set up activities and habits that encourage us to stop and take a look around, rather than blindly rushing from point A to point B. At its core, mindfulness concerns focusing on the present and experiencing the moment fully. Being mindful slows you down. It gives you room to breathe. When you engage in mindfulness, you are allowing yourself to notice where and when you can add meaning and magic to your everyday life.

The key to practicing mindfulness is to be deliberate about it. Choose an activity that you engage in daily and do it mindfully. You can start with something like your daily skincare routine or eating breakfast. While you are doing the activity, start an inner monologue stating what it is that you are doing. For example, narrate the entire process of eating from when you get hungry ("I'm feeling hunger pains in my stomach"), to getting your food ("I am choosing to eat a donut because it is the easiest thing I can eat right now"), to actually eating the food ("I am eating the donut").

This might sound like the opposite of magical in that it is an unimaginative retelling of what is going on, but it breaks down the activity of eating from one action into several smaller steps. Each one offers an opportunity to include magic. You can then decide where you want to add purpose and meaning to different aspects of the activity. Perhaps you want to include choosing foods that have magical properties, so you add a bit of cinnamon to the donut. Or maybe you decide you want to add an act of gratitude to your meal and give a word of thanks before you start eating. It is easier to see where you can add in these little touches of purposefulness to your meal when you are mindful.

Gratitude

There have been multiple studies on the role gratitude plays in people's mental and physical health.[17] All signs point to the fact that gratitude can make people happier, reduce stress and anxiety,

17. Maureen Salamon, "Gratitude Enhances Health, Brings Happiness—and May Even Lengthen Lives," Harvard Health Publishing, September 11, 2024, https://www.health.harvard.edu/blog/gratitude-enhances-health-brings-happiness-and-may-even-lengthen-lives-202409113071; Erika Stoerkel, "The Science and Research on Gratitude and Happiness," PositivePsychology.com, February 4, 2019, https://positivepsychology.com/gratitude-happiness-research/.

and aid in depression. Gratitude has the added benefit of playing a role in giving purpose to your life.

Gratitude can buoy you when times are tough. It can also aid you in problem-solving, as you can identify resources that you can tap into when you are in need. When expressing gratitude, think beyond the physical to your emotional and magical blessings. If nothing else, you can be thankful that you are a witch who has access to a whole range of ways to solve your problems.

Gratitude can take on many forms. The most well-known is counting one's blessings. This can be done at any time, but it can be the most helpful when you are facing stress. Reminding yourself of what you have can help counteract the negative emotions you're feeling when you are faced with a problem.

Another way to incorporate gratitude into your life is to give thanks. This is different from saying thanks reactively whenever the situation calls for it. Instead, you pause before saying the word and think about what it really means. You can also give thanks in situations where it usually isn't used. For example, whenever I divine, I tell my tarot cards thank you after I have finished the reading. I am thankful for the insight they have given me and want to let them know it. This also strengthens the bond I have with my cards, meaning I will continue to get helpful advice from them as the years go on.

Finally, you can spread your gratitude. Telling friends and family that you are thankful for them amplifies the blessings of their love and friendship. This will strengthen already established ties. You are also sending out into the universe your thanks for those relationships.

Building Relationships

I've discussed a couple of times in *A Witch Is* that community and relationships are important when it comes to magic. Witches understand that they are part of a larger whole, which includes not only other people but nature and the universe around us. So when I mention building relationships in this section, I'm referring to all the various kinds of relationships one can have. This includes connections to the genii locorum, plant and crystal allies, helper spirits, and deities. These relationships offer us connection as well as support, opportunities for learning, and even aid in our magical efforts.

Look at your relationships and consider the meaning behind them. Are you spending time with people who lift you up and make you happy? Or are your relationships toxic? What do you get out of them? And what do you offer in return? Know that it is okay to look at a friendship or a relationship with a family member and realize that it is harmful to you. In those cases, you want to limit your exposure to those people or cut them off altogether. While that might be difficult to start, you'll find that you are happier in the long run.

Relationships can also be short-term. This is especially true for ones that are teacher-student relationships. In this case, you work together until it is no longer necessary and then say your goodbyes. I have had this with various deities over the years. I once worked with Hecate for a year and a day. When the time was up, we both knew that I no longer needed the help and knowledge she had to give. I said thank you and we went our separate ways. If your relationship comes to a natural conclusion, you can feel grateful for what you shared and learned and go on to the next one.

Living a purposeful life is simply a matter of taking the time to pay attention to what is going on inside and around you. In your mindfulness and gratitude, you are looking at things differently. With your relationships, you are making sure that they are healthy and supportive rather than tearing you down. And should you come across anything that doesn't serve you, you let it go to make room for those things that will make you happy and fill your life with meaning.

EXERCISES

It is essential to make the time to consider how you do the things you do. This can seem counterintuitive to many people. It might even seem to discourage spontaneity. However, by planning things out ahead of time, you actually make it easier to make decisions because you already know how you should act in any given situation.

The following exercises are set up to help you make a blueprint for your pre-spellcasting ritual and to expand your astral residence so that things you'll need will already be in place for your use. Spend time on each, playing around with what you would like to do for your ritual and what you would like to see in your astral residence. And if you find, after putting them into practice, that an aspect or the whole thing doesn't work for you, begin again. You can always change things up after you have tried them.

Creating a Pre-Spellcasting Ritual

YOU'LL NEED:

- Your book of shadows (if you keep one), a few sheets of paper, or even the Notes app on your phone
- Something to write with

In this exercise, you are going to build a ritual to perform before you cast spells. By creating it now, when you aren't already engaged in working some magic, you'll have it on hand for when you need it.

Think about what you would like to do before you cast a spell. Do you feel like you'd need to cleanse yourself? How would you set up your space? What would you do to indicate that it is a workspace? Would you cast a circle? Strike a bell? Light incense or a candle? Would you like to invite helper spirits or deities into your workspace?

Spend some time thinking about how your pre-spellcasting ritual will feel to you. What emotions do you want it to evoke? How we feel before, during, and after a spell is just as important as the actions we take. You want to feel confident and self-assured, as that will translate into a better, more productive spell than if you are self-conscious and unsure. This is the benefit of planning your pre-spellcasting ritual out ahead of time: it will help you feel more at ease when you are performing it.

Write out what your pre-spellcasting ritual would be. Or, if you are more artistically inclined, draw it out. Once you have decided on what you want you pre-spellcasting ritual to look like, you are going to add the aftercare steps that you created in the "Spell Aftercare" exercise on page 93. By doing this, you have created a full ritual that you can use for any spellwork.

Expanding on Your Astral Residence

We return to the astral residence in this exercise. By now, you should have gone to it at least a couple of times to work magic, meditate, do shadow work, or do some other magical activity. If you haven't, this is as good a time as any to get started. You are going to spend some time building the tools you need in your astral residence so that they are always there when you need them.

Start by entering your astral residence in the way you are accustomed to, whether this is through the stairway method or another that you have decided on. You are going to create four places there. The spots you create will give you access to the earth, fire, air, and water elements. You will also create an altar that you can work at. All of this will require your visualization ability. Feel free to play around with aspects of each element to find the one that best suits your astral residence. These can change at any time as well, so you are not stuck with your first creation if it ends up not really working for you.

Start with earth. This should be the easiest for you to access because you have to stand on something in your astral residence. Envision a spot of earth, a boulder, a rocky outcropping, or a mound somewhere inside or around your astral residence. My own residence is housed in a cabin in the woods, so in order to access the earth element, I must go outside of it into the garden that I have planted next to the cabin. This is where you can ground; gather soil, rocks, or earth energies for spellwork; and engage with any earth spirits that might take up residence there. Get into as much detail as you can, imagining how it will smell and feel when you touch it.

Next, move on to the fire element. In my astral residence, I have a large fireplace where I can light fires. You might want to do the same if your residence is in a building, or you might have a camp circle where you can start a flame. You might, instead, envision a single or multiple candles, a torch, or even a flow of lava. The benefit of the astral residence is that you cannot be hurt there, so if you want to imagine that you access fire energies by dipping your hand into a volcano, you can do so.

For the air element, you can access the air around you. You might want to envision a clifftop or a platform at the top of a tree. It can be a tower or a lighthouse. The point is to create a space where you will be up high and can feel the breeze on your face. This can be a bit intimidating to people who have a fear of heights, as I do. This is where, again, you keep in mind that you can't be hurt in your astral residence. If you were to fall from your air element station, you can simply fly or float to the ground.

For water, I have a well just outside of my cabin that I can use. You might want to use a more natural water source, however: a stream, a pond, or even an ocean. Whatever you decide on, you should be able to access the water easily, so make sure you have a way to get to it. This will serve you whenever you need water or water energies for your spellwork. The water can also be used for cleansing yourself and your space before you begin your magic. I tend to pull up a bucket of water and use it to mop the floor and wash the altar of my astral residence before I start a spell.

Finally, you need to set up an altar. This is where you will cast all your magic when you are in your astral residence. Mine is a simple, long wooden table in the middle of my cabin. But you can create whatever your heart desires—all the fancy, witchy items that you can't afford in your physical life, you can have here. Go all out, creating a space that puts you in the mood for magic.

Once you have created these five places in your astral residence, put them to use. Grab fire to light under a cauldron full of water. Pull down wind to fuel your spells for creativity and intellect. Place crystals taken from your earth spot onto your altar to help amplify your intentions. Working with them regularly will only make them stronger.

A Witch Is Honest

Honesty, we're told, is the best policy. And yet we see lies everywhere we look, from the small fibs in advertising to the larger falsehoods peddled by politicians. Honesty is often meant for others, not the people telling the lies. It can get to the point where we feel like we have to hide the truth just to get along in society.

However, when it comes to magic, lying can have disastrous effects. If we are not honest with what we want, who we are dealing with, and what our beliefs are, then our magic will either have to work harder to overcome the falsehoods or deliver something we didn't actually want.

This doesn't mean that those who have to hide their magic are in the wrong. The world can be a dangerous place to those of us who walk a different path from the majority. We'll discuss later in this chapter what to do when you need to hide what you are doing from others.

Your Intentions

Honesty with yourself is one of the most important traits for a witch. Magic is fueled by intention, and if you aren't honest with yourself, that can screw up your spellcasting. Dishonesty can come in many shapes and forms when we're dealing with feelings about ourselves. Doubt can creep into our magic when we spend more time focused on our failings than our strengths. While it might seem to make sense that we acknowledge both, we can give outsized importance to those ways we are weak and diminish our strengths. To counteract this, go back to your magical strengths and weaknesses that you identified on page 122. For every weakness you think you have, determine a strength. This way you have a balance and an answer for whenever your brain throws up an objection to why you can't accomplish something. For every "I can't do this because I am bad at this," you'll have a counterargument.

One obstacle can be the feeling that you don't deserve what you are striving for. If you lack self-confidence but are performing spells for things like love, money, respect at work, etc., the disconnect between what you want and what you think you deserve will undermine your efforts. The idea of "fake it till you make it" doesn't work with magic. You need to work on setting up your magic to take into account the drag your negative self-belief causes to your work.

The solution is not to ignore the issue but to face it head on. You can consult chapter 13 for ways to do so. For now, though, you are going to be honest with yourself. What is getting in the way of you living the fully realized magical life you want? Maybe you don't believe you deserve abundance, respect, or love. In that case, there are two ways you can deal with that issue, but first, you are going to have to admit to that as you consider your spellcasting.

The first way to deal with feelings of unworthiness is to move the focus from yourself to your actions. Our society believes that hard work deserves to be rewarded. And while we can argue whether that is true in practice in a capitalistic society, you can use that belief to your advantage. You are putting in the work, so it should reap benefits. You want to remove yourself and your negative self-esteem from the magical equation. Instead of focusing on what you believe you don't deserve, you are going to think about what it is that you do to accomplish your goals.

It can be difficult to remove yourself when you are working magic. The ego wants us to be at the forefront of everything we do. Mindfulness can help with this. As you cast the spell, you can engage the inner monologue outlining what you are doing, rather than what you are feeling. This is much like following an unfamiliar recipe, when you concentrate on the ingredients and steps so much that you don't have time to worry if it will turn out. Keep reminding yourself that you are doing the hard work and that results will follow.

Another, albeit more difficult, method is to acknowledge your feelings in your spellcasting. Phrase your spells in such a way that you are enacting the change you want despite yourself. This is taking into account your sense of not deserving what you desire and reframing it as yet another obstacle to overcome, rather than leaving it to work against you in the background. By dragging your feelings of unworthiness into the forefront you are taking control of the narrative your brain is making up. This makes your spellcasting have to face that hurdle along with all the others it has to contend with. Which can mean it might take longer for results to manifest, or that you might have to put in extra effort to support your spellwork. The more you face your own self-sabotaging thoughts, however, the less power they will hold over you.

The flip side of feeling like we don't deserve what we want is not being honest with ourselves about our desires. This disconnect might not undermine your magic, but it is likely to deliver results you don't want. If, for example, you cast a love spell looking for a partner with qualities you *think* you should find attractive rather than what you truly want, you can end up with someone who you aren't happy with.

Magic supports mundane actions and vice versa.

This is where you need to be brutally honest with yourself before you start your work. Before you engage in a spell, you need to think about what it is you really want. You can turn to divination to see if you have any blind spots related to the task at hand. Journal about what you want, how you expect it to show up, and what actions you will take to secure it outside of the spell. Be honest with yourself throughout the exercise, especially on that last part. If you aren't willing to do the physical work, the magical isn't going to help. Magic supports mundane actions and vice versa.

Being honest with yourself is one of those times when you are truly vulnerable. None of us is a perfect creature, and so we need to give ourselves grace when it comes to confronting our intentions. We can be selfish if we want and cast magic solely for our own benefit. And that's okay. One cannot pour from an empty glass, and there are many times when we need to take care of ourselves first. As long as we are clear about why we are doing what we are doing, we won't be making our magic work harder than it needs to in order to be successful.

When You Have to Hide the Truth

As a witchy author living in a deeply conservative state, I often find myself at odds when asked what I do for a living. It's not that I am ashamed of my books and my work, but that I have to consider my safety first and foremost. My answer to that question can often range from "I write about witchcraft" to "I write books about crafting and religion." It depends on my assessment of the person asking the question. Which brings us to one of the aspects of honesty: being honest does not mean telling everyone everything or being open if that isn't in your best interest.

There are many reasons a witch might be less than forthcoming, the first being the disapproval of friends and family. Having been raised Baptist, I learned very quickly that expressing an interest in magic and the occult was frowned upon. It would be years before I was in a place where I felt comfortable being my authentic, witchy self. Many more people are not in a place where they can be so. In those cases, it is absolutely fine to keep your beliefs and practices to yourself. There are ways you can do so that won't alert family, friends, or housemates. Remember, it is intention that is the core of magic and witchcraft, so an altar can just look like a collection of items, a houseplant can serve as a source of protection, or you can hide powders and spell pouches in out-of-the way places where no one will notice.

The astral residence can help in keeping your practice safe from prying eyes, as all the magic happens in your mind. However, there are other ways to practice covert magic. The first is to enchant everyday objects. You can charm the jewelry or clothes that you wear for everyday protection. To protect your home or space, charge a wreath or a statue with protective properties. Even a small toy, stone, or painting can be used to provide protection:

simply enchant it and then place it near the entrance of the space you want to protect.

Engage in magic that looks like something different, such as kitchen or green witchery. Your practice will look like cooking or gardening to the unknowing eye. If you can't use tarot cards or runes, try a form of divination like bibliomancy. This is where you interpret a random passage drawn from a book. Traditionally, the Bible is used in bibliomancy, but any text that is sacred to you would work. In this way, it looks only like you are reading rather than practicing witchcraft.

You can also use more mundane versions of witchcraft items. For example, use tea lights or container candles instead of pillar or chime candles for candle magic. Use an aromatic tea in place of incense. Use a song you like for cleansing instead of lighting up a smoke bundle so that people just think you are enjoying music. If you put your mind to it, you should be able to figure out ways to cast spells without arousing suspicion.

While most of society has become more open and accepting of witchcraft and Paganism over the last few decades, there is always a risk with living your life out in the open. Employers can discriminate in a myriad of ways that won't attract the attention of labor boards. Every year there are stories of metaphysical shops being vandalized by religious fanatics. There are still parts of the world where being labeled a witch can lead to an individual being harmed or even killed. With that in mind, you should not feel bad about taking precautions for your own safety if you need to.

Additionally, witches are not required to spill all their secrets when it comes to how they practice their craft. With the advent of WitchTok, Witches of Instagram, and other groups, social media is often flooded with images and videos of spellwork. There's been discussion on whether or not this is a good thing. Showing your working, from start to finish, with a description of everything that went into the spell might help others learn how to cast spells and work magic. However, it also gives those watching the power to thwart your spell. In an age when some people spend all their time being trolls on the internet, it's not too far-fetched to believe there will be some witches who try to subvert others' spells just for shits and giggles.

As someone who has posted my spells on Instagram and YouTube, I take precautions not to show everything. I write generalized descriptions of my workings. And I don't post about them until after I have seen some sort of result. I will omit ingredients as well if they are particularly personal to me. Yes, it requires me to suppress my ego and sidestep the desire for instant gratification that likes and follows bring. But it is a small price to pay to safeguard my witchcraft in today's digital age.

You shouldn't have to hide who you are, but your safety has to be a number one priority. If you have to keep your practice on the down-low, I hope that one day you can be out and proud. In the meantime, I hope that you can practice in peace.

It may seem simplistic to state that honesty is the best policy, but I believe it is true. That's not to say there aren't times when you should keep the truth close to your chest. But for the most part, being honest—with others and with yourself—will serve you best.

EXERCISES

Being true to yourself is the fundamental outcome of being honest with yourself. The following exercises are meant to help you uncover what it is that you truly believe and where you draw the line when it comes to magic. Approach both exercises with an open mind and the intent to engage with them honestly, and you'll find that you have a better understanding of what makes you tick.

Truth or Dare

YOU'LL NEED:

- Your book of shadows (if you keep one), a few sheets of paper, or even the Notes app on your phone
- Something to write with

There are types of magic that we are unwilling to engage in. This may be love magic, if we feel that the chance of overriding someone's free will is a no-go area for ourselves. This might be necromancy, if we don't feel comfortable talking with the dead. Whatever the type of magic is, we should know what our red lines are before we proceed further into our practice.

This exercise is meant to get to the heart of the types of magic that go against your ethics. This is not a condemnation of those types of magic. In the instance of love magic, many of the spells that were meant to tie lovers together can be traced back to the magic of enslaved Africans in the United States to keep husbands and wives faithful after they had been sold off. This falls under the umbrella of magic that requires cultural and historical perspective. Witches need to decide for themselves what magic they are willing to engage in without judgment of others who might work magic that they would not.

You are going to engage in an episode of truth or dare in deciding what magic you will engage in and what magic you will forgo. This is tied to your honesty with yourself. Don't go along with magic that you don't condone just because you think you should. If you don't feel comfortable with a type of magic, then you shouldn't engage in it. But if a magical working piques your interest, then perhaps you should explore it a little further, reading up on how it is worked to see if it is something you should add to your practice.

Consider the following types of magic, but don't feel like you need to stick solely to this list. If you already have an idea of magic that you don't think you would like to engage in, add that to the list to write about.

- Love magic, specifically magic meant to make someone fall in love with you or to keep your lover faithful
- Necromancy, summoning and talking with the dead
- Hexing, targeting a person with your magic to cause bad things to happen to them
- Sexual magic, in which the magic is fueled by the energies raised by sexual touch and orgasms
- Blood magic or any other bodily fluid (yours or others') magic
- Working with destructive deities such as Kali, Tiamat, Lilith, Hel, Nyx, Anubis, and Loki

Write down if you would work with the above magic and why or why not. Try to go beyond the gut reaction of "It doesn't appeal to me." Dig deep and figure out why you have the reaction you do. If you find that some of the magic above interests you, then write out why you think that is. Consider how you might work it into your magical practice. Reflect on how your approach to these magics is fueled by your own personal beliefs and ethics.

Let your thoughts sit for a month or so and then return to your writings and see if your attitude has changed at all toward any of the practices you were not interested in. During that time, research and try your hand at magic that interests you and then write down what you have learned.

Your Personal Mission Statement

YOU'LL NEED:

- Your book of shadows (if you keep one), a few sheets of paper, or even the Notes app on your phone
- Something to write with

Many of your decisions, both magic and mundane, are guided by your belief system. In this exercise, you are going to sit down and write out a sort of personal mission statement, which will encompass what you believe in. You can then use it to make decisions and speak from your core.

You want to start by writing down all the things that are important to you. These can be things like kindness, learning, having control of your life, and so on. They can also be things you do, like reading, helping others, and going out with friends. This is your personal mission statement, so you want it to reflect what is important to you, not what you think should be important. Don't let the need to look good to others get in the way of writing from the heart.

Next, you are going to write down your goals. What is it that you want to accomplish in life? What would your ideal life look like? What would you be doing? Think about what it is that you truly want out of life. Write down everything, again focusing on what you really want, rather than what you think you should be doing. This can include "selfish" goals that benefit only you. We are allowed to think about ourselves just as much as we think of other people.

Now you are going to put those two lists together to create your mission statement. Start with phrases like "I believe…" or "I will…" and add in what is important to you and how those help you achieve your goals. A mission statement doesn't need to be long. In fact, the shorter the better, as it will be easier to remember. A sentence can encapsulate your beliefs and goals succinctly.

Some examples of mission statements are as follows:

- "I believe in my ability to change and grow, and my mission is to develop myself through the application of magic and knowledge."
- "I will use my talents for magic to help those who need it, including myself, in alignment with my beliefs of kindness and charity."
- "My love for myself means that I will always put myself first."
- "My goal is to provide safety and support for myself, my friends, and my family."
- "I will make decisions and choices based on my beliefs of justice, fairness, and equity."

Once you have written your mission statement, put it somewhere you will see it often. When you are faced with difficulties or have to make a decision, refer back to your mission statement to help guide you. When you need to perform a spell or other kind of magic, you can make sure that it aligns with your personal beliefs.

A Witch Is Respectful

Respect is one of those concepts that has become contentious in recent years. This is due to the word having been co-opted to mean "being treated like an authority." Those who use that meaning do so to oppress those who they believe should grant them respect automatically. No wonder one might bristle at the idea that to be a witch is to be respectful.

But I use the word in its original meaning of regard for the rights, feelings, and thoughts of others. Although it does have to do with interpersonal relationships, it focuses on finding common ground rather than engaging in a power struggle. I wrote about how the witch is connected to everything in "The Interconnectedness of the World" in chapter 4. This fact requires witches to acknowledge that their place in the world is neither above nor below other beings.

Whether people, animals, spirits, or deities, all beings deserve the bare minimum of respect until they prove themselves unworthy of it. That is to say that we approach the greater world around us acknowledging its right to exist. Our respect needs to extend not only to the land and other cultures but also to ourselves. If we don't regard ourselves with dignity, it can affect our magic.

Of the Land and Spirits

There is a tendency for people to take a domination mindset when it comes to land. This is tied into feelings of ownership, competition, and protectionism. For witches in the United States, this is exacerbated by concepts like the American dream, colonialism, and manifest destiny, which were drivers of early American expansion to the detriment of the native populations who already lived here. These concepts of domination and ownership shaped the way we think of the land we now occupy. Owning a home or land, we're taught, is freedom. It is power. It is something we should all desire, we're told.

This attitude sets us on a path that conflicts with our beliefs as witches. Witchcraft is rooted in nature and the world around us. How can we claim ownership over something that we recognize as a living entity? How can we especially sustain the idea of ownership when we, as Americans, live on stolen land?

The thing is, the idea of ownership is tied to the ego in many ways. That belief, that owning something brings with it power, can be very seductive. In a society where the gap between the weak and the powerful is at a historical high, we long for something that can help us feel safe. But in a world where the government can seize property through eminent domain, where so many of us are living paycheck to paycheck and are only one bad month away from homelessness, that sense of safety is an illusion.

I learned this lesson firsthand when I lost my house in 2018. My family and I were homeless, separated from each other, for a couple of months. And though we managed to find a place relatively quickly, I realized how precarious our situation was and never got that sense of stability back. Even if you are secure in your housing, you should be aware that circumstances can force you out of your place.

The point of all this is not to alarm you but to illustrate that a witch must have a different attitude toward the land they reside on. The land, and its spirits, deserve our respect, as they will still be here long after we are gone.

This is why I say a witch is respectful of the land they occupy and the spirits who live there. Rather than viewing ourselves as owners of the land, we can take the view that we are its stewards. This means being part of its conservation for future generations. It also means lending your magic and energy to the land and its spirits.

Start with mundane actions such as picking up litter in areas you frequent. You can also send healing energy to the land in the same way that you ground. Send the roots from your feet into the earth and then send white, healing light into it. Ask for nothing in return. Also, learn about the land you are on and its legal status. Find out what local laws govern the land. All this information will guide your approach to the land. For example, public areas may have rules about foraging, so you want to be aware of them before you head out to collect materia magica. Keep in mind that certain areas, like sacred sites, shouldn't be foraged from. They are visited by so many people that if each person took only one rock, leaf, scoop of dirt, or flower, it would soon be stripped bare.

Locating Local Land Spirits

Having a good relationship with the local land spirits around you gives you access to their wisdom and aid. Before you can connect with them, you have to find them first. This can feel tricky, especially if you live in a place that is disconnected from the land such as an apartment or in the city. Even then, however, you can find spirits to work with, if you only listen.

Start with divination. Using whatever divination form you are most comfortable with, ask about the local spirits: what their temperament is like, if they are open to working with you, how you should approach them. This lays the groundwork for your next steps.

Remember that the spirit is as much an individual as you are.

Work at your altar or in a space where you won't be interrupted. If you choose to do this outside of your home in a park, the woods, or your backyard, you can do things like put in earbuds and sit on a blanket to look like you are meditating. Make sure you are always aware of your surroundings, however. You will need some sandalwood incense, as sandalwood is beneficial in summoning spirits. Light your incense and arrange yourself comfortably in a seated or standing position.

Start by listening intently to the area around you. Make note of any ambient sounds you hear, if there is noise like dogs barking, people talking, or the morning garbage pickup. Let those sounds drift out of your attention. You are establishing what the environment sounds and feels like before you actively reach out to a spirit.

Send out an unspoken invitation to whatever spirits are around. Make sure to extend the invitation to those spirits who are interested in having a relationship with you. Sit quietly and note any differences in the area now that you have reached out. Maybe there is a change in the air temperature, or the birds stop singing or get louder. Perhaps you feel the presence of a spirit. Look for signs while maintaining your quiet listening.

Once you have ascertained a spirit's presence, ask it its name and give yours. Let it know what you are looking for and what you are willing to do in return for aid and information. The answers may come as feelings, images in your mind, or even a small voice near you. The response will depend on the spirit. If the spirit agrees to work with you, thank it. You can continue to talk to the spirit at that point or let it go. If you are working out of doors, make sure to clean up the area from anything you brought out for the meeting, such as spent incense.

Now that you have made a connection with a local land spirit, make sure you uphold your end of the bargain, making offerings and providing energy if that is the promise you made. Remember that the spirit is as much an individual as you are, so treat it with respect for its efforts, knowledge, and time. If you do so, you will have made an ally for life.

Of Other Cultures and Magical Practices

Modern witchcraft has a problem. It was built on the research and insight of a handful of white British and American witches and those in the New Age movement who had no issue with plundering various other cultures for their practices. Some examples include the use of white sage and smudging from various Native American cultures, who were not legally allowed to engage in such practices in the United States until 1978.[18] With the turn of the century, we had a shift in attitude, leading to witches starting to try to decolonize their witchcraft and grow their understanding of concepts like cultural appropriation and closed practices.

18. "1978: American Indian Freedom of Religion Legalized," Native Voices, National Library of Medicine, accessed May 27, 2025, https://www.nlm.nih.gov/nativevoices/timeline/545.html.

As a witch, especially if you are a white person, the onus is on you to make sure that your craft does no harm when it comes to other cultures and magical practices. In many indigenous cultures, people were legally restricted from practicing their own religions. And yet white practitioners would adopt elements of those same religions and insert them into their "eclectic" practice without any consequence. This is neither a compassionate nor a kind witchcraft.

Making your practice less harmful can be a deeply upsetting process, as it can bring up feelings of guilt, annoyance, and even anger. That is understandable but not a reason to avoid doing the work. Those emotions come from a misplaced sense of ownership, which is a disrespectful approach to witchcraft.

So what can you do to make sure that your practice is being respectful of others? You need to decolonize your practice and beliefs, vet your sources, and do shadow work if necessary to deal with the feelings that are brought up along the way. You also need to be aware of practices that might be closed to you because you don't come from the culture, and you need to be okay with that.

Decolonize Your Practice

To decolonize your practice is to have one that is free from the cultural and psychological effects of colonization. This means interrogating your practice to see if it contains anything that belongs to indigenous populations. Do the research into your own family history to see if you have any legitimate claims to those cultures and if you don't, cut those activities out of your practice. Read books, blog posts, and social media of indigenous and non-white witches, such as Juliet Diaz, Lorraine Monteagut, Elhoim Leafar, Dra. Rocío, and Benebell Wen, among others, to learn about how to decolonize your practice, while keeping in mind that each person is an individual and not the spokesperson for their entire group. You are looking for consensus on what members of particular cultures consider proprietary to their group and what isn't.

If you come across a tradition that resonates with you but belongs to a closed practice (meaning that it is not available for outsiders), respect that. You can do research to see if there are similar practices in other cultures that are open to you. For example, instead of white sage, smoke bundles of rosemary, lavender, or cedar can be used to cleanse a space without fear of appropriation.

Make sure you are vetting your sources when you come across new knowledge, especially when it comes to information shared on social media. If you come across a piece of magic that claims to be from a particular path or practice, do a web search to see if you can confirm the claim. Check to see if people who provide knowledge and information have credentials or experience.

Also, if you are going to learn about or participate in a practice that is centered on a culture not your own, make sure you find teachers who are part of that culture. The same goes for supplies and items. Find local, cultural artisans and supplies. For example, if you wish to have a dream catcher, buy one from an Ojibwe artisan rather than from Amazon. You are then not only supporting the culture the item comes from but respecting it.

Do the (Shadow) Work

It can be difficult to find out that there are some kinds of witchcraft and magic that are not available to you. If, like me, you come from a Christian upbringing, this can be especially true, as that religion is presented as one that is open to all.[19] It can also be hard for

19. This ignores the fact that the way Christianity has been spread is often violent, forcing people to convert or face discrimination or even death, with many people given no real option to not join.

white Americans who were brought up on the belief of freedom for all, meaning that everything is available for everyone. We can feel unjustly excluded. As a Gen X witch, I grew up with the belief that "information wants to be free." And it took years for me to understand that not everything is for me to engage in, and that is okay.

Since this shadow work is going to dig into some powerful, possibly negative emotions, I recommend that you do it when you have set up a space that is protective and conducive to doing the work. Create protective space by drawing a circle around it, lighting white candles, or placing some amethyst next to you. Next, burn an incense mixture of one part mugwort (to access the deeper parts of your mind) to one part rosemary (for its protective and mental properties). Finally, ground and center yourself before you start.

Use your book of shadows, if you keep one, or your journal to work through whatever feelings come up when you are faced with closed practices. What emotions are brought up? Ask yourself why you feel the way you do. Don't flinch away from the answers that come up. Write down everything. It may be that you find some of your feelings or thoughts are rooted in racism, which can be very upsetting. In these cases, remember that we live in a society that is built on racism and has it baked into its structure. It is impossible not to have that impact us in negative ways. Being aware of those emotions and beliefs is the first step to getting rid of them.

Once you've done this work, keep the information close at hand for when you are researching and learning about magical practices. If a knee-jerk reaction of anger, frustration, or annoyance comes up, you can return to your writings to remind yourself that these are emotions from your shadow self. You can acknowledge that you are feeling them, and then let them go.

Of Themselves

There are any number of concerns and conditions that can plague the witch throughout their practice. There are doubts about whether the magic will work or not and worries that we're not working magic in the "right" way. All of these can work against us. But all of them can be hard to dismiss right away because self-sabotage is insidious, popping up when we least expect it. We can deal with those bothersome issues by remembering that we are worthy of respect, educating ourselves, and having a good sense of who we are and what we stand for.

By now you should have a good understanding of who you are as a witch and your path. You've written a personal mission statement. You've explored different types of magic to see which ones are attuned to you as a person. And you've built a personal set of correspondences to suit your magical needs. You've done the work and established just what kind of witch you are. That is worthy of celebration and respect.

Another way to respect yourself is to practice magic that aligns with your beliefs. This is why going through the exercises to define what you believe in has been worthwhile. When you know what you stand for, you can make better decisions and honor yourself. Look over what you have done in the past and count your successes. Know that you have done great things before and that you will do them again in the future. You should be proud of the work you have done already.

Self-respect is an aspect of self-love. When you treat yourself with respect, you are showing others how they should treat you.

This goes for fellow people as well as spirits, deities, and any other powers you might work with. To that end, if you find that you don't have respect for yourself, you can work on that magically.

Magic for Self-Respect

There are several ways to support your journey to self-respect. Herbs like lavender, rosemary, and chamomile can promote inner peace, which allows for self-reflection and healing. Drink a tea made from any or all of these herbs before you engage in divination on your inner self. Carrying a crystal like malachite opens you up for change so that you can work on respecting yourself, whereas carrying bloodstone will grant you the courage for change.

Self-Love Spell Pouch

You'll need:

- Small pouch of blue fabric, for its healing energies
- Piece of rhodochrosite
- Dried rose petals
- Dried lavender buds
- Small piece of paper and something to write with

I also recommend having music on in the background that makes you feel good. You could always queue up Aretha Franklin's classic "Respect" to get into the right frame of mind.

Start by creating sacred, working space in whatever way you are most comfortable. Next, place the rhodochrosite into the pouch and say, "I love myself." See pink or green light coming from your heart and filling the pouch along with the crystal. Next, place the rose petals into the pouch and say, "I respect myself." See blue light coming from your throat and filling the pouch alongside the petals. Add in the lavender buds and say, "I believe in myself." See purple light coming from your head and joining the buds inside the pouch.

Now, using your writing utensil, draw a heart on the small piece of paper. Place the slip of paper into the pouch while saying, "I love and respect and believe in myself." Carry the pouch with you, taking it in hand whenever you feel like you need to remind yourself that you are worthy of respect, especially your own.

The Altar of Respect

This can be built and used whenever you need a boost to your self-esteem and self-respect. You will basically build an altar to yourself. On your altar, place photos of yourself that you like. Add in any awards or recognitions you have received over the years. If you haven't received any awards, make some up for yourself. Write out what you have accomplished over the years, the magic you have engaged in, your degrees or accomplishments you have made on the job—even a "World's Best Pet Parent" mug can be added to the altar. Set flowers that you like on the altar. Place a candle in your favorite color. Burn incense that makes you feel good. Have an offering on hand. This can be a small piece of chocolate, a shot of alcohol, a cookie, or just a glass of water. It should be something you enjoy.

You aren't worshiping yourself but giving yourself honor.

Now that you have set up your altar, you are going to use it in the same way you would an altar for an ancestor, deity, or other spirit. You aren't necessarily worshiping yourself but giving yourself honor. Light the candle on your altar. Breathe in and let your eyes wander over all the photos, art, and other objects that you have gathered there. Let them fill you with feelings of love and gratitude. Consider your many accomplishments, no matter how small they are. Perhaps all you did today was feed yourself. Give yourself praise for having done so. Think about how far you have come from your early days in magic to now, where you stand before an altar built to your own magnificence. You are someone worthy of praise.

Give yourself the offering. Tell yourself, "I make this offering to myself because I am worth it." Eat or drink your offering and savor it. You are worthy of respect. Think of all the things you will accomplish in the future because you are aligned with your goals and capable of magic great and small. Once you have finished your offering, thank yourself. Give thanks for the body you inhabit. Give thanks for your mind, which has brought you this far. Give thanks for your heart and feelings, which have guided you throughout your life. And give thanks for your magic, which has the power to change your life for the better.

Once you have given thanks, extinguish the candle. Go back to this altar time and again until you start to believe in yourself and respect yourself when you are away from the altar. You can keep some of the photos and lists of accomplishments in your journal or book of shadows, if you keep one, to refer back to whenever you feel your self-respect falter. This is a process, and it might take time for you to see results, but don't give up.

Of Their Power

Magic is powerful. As the saying goes, "With great power comes great responsibility." As a witch, you have to be willing to face the consequences of your magic. This means making sure to limit any potential unintended consequences, ensuring the magic is targeted and protecting yourself when you cast your magic.

As a witch, you have a great responsibility to use your power. Whether it is for good or ill, for better or worse, is up to you. But you need to recognize that the power inside you needs to be exercised, or it will wither. I am the first person who will encourage witches to look for a magical approach to problems they face. Throughout *A Witch Is*, I have suggested affirmations, divination, spells, and rituals to tackle issues. I believe that adding magic to the mix can help us overcome the steepest of obstacles. However, I do also believe that we must not treat magic carelessly.

This isn't to say that we cannot cast magic for selfish reasons or that our magic has to be high-minded and worked only for the "greater good." Working spells for your own self-enrichment is a completely acceptable use of your magic. Working magic for small things, such as trying to get all green lights so your commute time is shorter, is okay.

You should be working magic that aligns with your values. This can mean that you might not be comfortable with spells that target individuals personally or that might cause any harm. I've known witches who don't like freezer spells or hexes for a variety of reasons. One witch I know who was plagued with an unpleasant colleague at work cast a spell to get that person a promotion so that they would be moved to a different department. Not wanting to harm anyone with one's magic is perfectly okay.

However, it is also okay to cast magic against others if they have harmed you first. In those cases, you need to make doubly sure that there won't be any collateral damage when it comes to your spells. We discussed this in "The Interconnectedness of the World" on page 67. This also includes making sure that you are targeting the right person with your magic. Usually, this is straightforward: the ex who won't leave you alone, the neighbor who keeps parking in your spot, the coworkers who gossip about you—all are easily identified. However, there are times you might be dealing with an unknown perpetrator, and in those cases, you will need to use other tools to identify them.

You also want to make sure that any spell targeting another person—whether to help or harm—is specific. This is where taglocks come into play. A taglock is a magical way of identifying someone in a spell. The most common taglocks are hair or fingernails, although they can also be just a person's name, their birthdate, or a photograph of them. The closer the taglock is to a person, the more ably a spell can target them. When it comes to spells meant to freeze or harm someone, you want to be as specific as possible. Fortunately, photographs are easier to come by in this day of social media than grabbing a hair or two off someone. When using a photo of someone for a spell, make sure that they are the only person in it.

If you don't know the person you are targeting in a spell (for example, if there is office gossip but you don't know who originated it), then a return to sender spell is a better use of your magic. In this spell, you are sending the malicious energy, negativity, and any harmful magic back to the person who is bothering you.

Return to Sender Spell

YOU'LL NEED:

- Charcoal disc, along with a fireproof container
- Pin or knife
- Black candle

- Small mirror
- Dried rue

Rue is a powerful hex-breaking herb. You will want to cast this spell during the waning moon to help weaken the negative energy that has been targeting you. Make sure to cast a protective circle around yourself and your space when you work this spell.

Place the charcoal disc in the fireproof container. Light a side of it with a match or lighter until it sparks and starts to burn. With a pin or knife tip, carve the word *Return* into the candle. Light it and place it so that the flame is reflected in the mirror. Take a pinch of the rue and drop it onto the charcoal while saying, "What you have sent my way I return to you." Visualize the negative energy that has been attacking you being returned to whoever sent it at you. Repeat this two more times, each time adding more rue to the charcoal disc.

Let the candle burn down and the charcoal disc extinguish. Once it has, take the ashes and mix them with sea salt. This will make a protective black salt that you can then sprinkle over your doorstep, inside your window frames, and down your drains and toilet. This will help keep the malicious energy from coming into your home. Carry a little bit of the ash on you in a small pouch until you feel like the spell has worked and you are no longer being targeted by the negative energy.

This spell can also be cast if you know who it is that is targeting you. When you are sending the energy back, just visualize the person.

~~~

You may have heard the statement "Respect is earned, not given." That is a very stingy way to look at the topic, in my opinion.
~~~

Everything, from other people to spirits to yourself, is deserving of basic respect. Without that, we are mean-spirited creatures, unable to form the most basic of connections with others. That doesn't mean that greater respect can't be withheld from those who prove themselves unworthy of it. We have the right to protect ourselves and our peace from those who would choose to attack us. What it does mean, however, is that you extend the most basic level of respect to others that you meet both in the mundane and the magical world. As a witch, whose magic affects the connections between you and the world around you, that respect smooths the way for your magic to be effective.

 EXERCISES 

The exercises that follow are two sides of the same coin. The first identifies those whom you respect and describes how you show it. The second allows you to view yourself as if you were the one being summoned and worked with. Both explore the idea of what it means to be respected when it comes to magic.

Working with Spirits, Deities, and Others

YOU'LL NEED:

- Your book of shadows (if you keep one), a few sheets of paper, or even the Notes app on your phone
- Something to write with

In this exercise, you are going to make a list of the spirits, deities, ancestors, and other beings you work with magically. Be sure to include your human mentors and mentees in the list. Next to each entry write a sentence about why you respect them. This could be as simple as "Because they give me advice on my magic," but you should be as detailed as possible. Really think about what you get from the relationship with each individual, how you define it, and what you offer in return.

If there are places where there are gaps, that's a sign that you need to reevaluate that relationship. Working with spirits or others that you don't respect will end up hurting you in the long run, as you will misstep and either offend them or get offended yourself. It is better to engage in relationships in which there is mutual understanding and trust. Make sure that the relationships are reciprocal and equitable.

Keep this list where you will be able to refer back to it so that you know whom you can count on when you need advice or knowledge.

Treat Yourself as an Ancestor

YOU'LL NEED:

- Your book of shadows (if you keep one), a few sheets of paper, or even the Notes app on your phone
- Something to write with

Sometimes you need to look at the big picture. This life that we lead will eventually end, and we will become an ancestor to our descendants. With that in mind, consider what kind of ancestor you would be. Write how you would be an ancestor to those who called upon you. Be as specific as possible. What knowledge would you pass along? What advice would you have to give? How would others show you respect? Even go so far as to consider what offerings you would want, how you would want to be summoned, and by whom.

A Witch Is Curious

In a 1952 letter to Carl Seelig, Albert Einstein wrote, "I have no special talents. I am only passionately curious."[20] This passion for curiosity is a key component of witchcraft. Without curiosity, we cannot see past the mundane into the magical, for one. Questioning everything is an important tool in the witch's toolbox.

A witch is curious because they don't accept the world how it is. Magic is a tool for change wielded most often to affect the world around us rather than for internal change. A witch doesn't look at the way things are and decide to let it be. Instead, they work to activate change through magical means.

Much like scientists, investigative journalists, and young children, witches are fueled by the questions "Why?" and "How?" How does the magical work and why does it work that way? We

20. Albert Einstein, *The Expanded Quotable Einstein,* ed. Alice Calaprice (Princeton University Press, 2000), 20.

dig deep into the world around us and try to make sense of it both mundanely and magically.

History is filled with curious witches who sought to commune with spirits and deities or who sought out the magical and medical properties of plants for healing. What they learned they passed on to others so that they might benefit from that wisdom. Witches were, and still are, curious about the world around them and how they can impact it through magic.

And this is why I say a witch is curious. A witch has to have the inborn curiosity to learn how to cast magic. Incurious people are satisfied with the way things are.

Curiosity is related to creative thinking, which in turn is related to problem-solving. When you are casting a spell, you are looking to solve a problem magically. Curiosity is what pushes us to find a solution rather than just living with the status quo.

Don't Accept the World as It Is

The fact that we look to change our fortune, or heal, or hurt, or in any other way have an impact on the world around us shows that witches are changemakers. We look at the world the way it is and decide, no, it can be different. We then attempt to make that change through magic and our actions. But before we can make those changes, we need to know exactly what is going on so that we will know how best to deal with the situation. This is an important part of the magic process, as you can't really address a situation until you have a good understanding of it. Looking into the what, who, where, when, and why of a situation will give you the answers you need.

There is a tendency to accept the status quo. As children, we are told not to "rock the boat." But as witches, we are supposed to do exactly that. Whenever you are faced with a situation, you must look past the surface and question why things are the way they are. Witches challenge the default by their very being. We see a situation and wonder how we could change it through magic.

Start by asking questions about everything you encounter. Why is something done a certain way? Who benefits from the way we do things? How can you benefit from a certain situation? How can you apply magic to the way things are? It's that last question that separates witches from others. We look to unseen and metaphysical solutions to problems. This isn't to say that every obstacle will be overcome by magic, but it shouldn't be a last resort.

I learned this lesson from my therapist, who is a witch and a Pagan herself. In therapy, as I outlined all the difficulties I was facing, she would ask, "Have you asked the cards about that?" or "Have you done a spell for that?" It threw me for a loop at first, to consider a magic solution to the most mundane of problems. But the more I thought about it, the more I realized it made sense for me. This way of thinking will come easier to some than to others. If you are one of those who doesn't naturally turn to magic when faced with an obstacle, it will take practice to get into the habit.

Turn to your divination tools when you have a problem and ask what you need to know about it or what tools you need to employ to address it. Meditate on the problem or situation and open yourself up to advice from your helper spirits and deities. Burn rosemary or peppermint incense to help you focus on the issue and to clear your mind so that you can come up with a solution. Hold a piece of pyrite while you think about your issue to help you dig deep for solutions.

Once you start questioning how you can use magic to help solve your problems, you'll find that your creativity and resilience start kicking in. Remember that magic will be supportive of your efforts; it is not a replacement for mundane actions. You still need to take your medications if you are on any, speak to professionals, and put yourself out there for resolutions to your issues.

Don't let yourself be thrown off by the unexpected. While being caught off-guard is natural when things don't go as planned, you can control how you react. Instead of being upset that the spell didn't work the way you wanted it to or that a spirit didn't respond when you reached out to it, ask "Why?"

And when challenging the status quo, don't get tangled up in ideas of being right. Magic is a tricky, twisting element that can contradict itself at various times. This is especially true when it comes to personal magic, where what might work for one person won't work for another. Being caught up in the idea that there is a right and a wrong way to work magic will just limit you. If something comes up that goes against what you have always believed, question it, but also question your beliefs.

Above all else, don't accept the world as it is. As a witch, you have the opportunity to change things so that they benefit you or others. So, question everything, challenge authority, and make your own case for why things should be different.

Curiosity and the Cat

There is a popular proverb: "Curiosity killed the cat." This is said as a caution against curiosity. Poke around, it warns, and one might be upset, and perhaps even actually harmed, by what one finds. In other words: "Fuck around and find out." However, that is only the first half of the proverb. The full quote is "Curiosity killed the cat. But satisfaction brought it back."

The curious instinct is not the end of the cat. The answers it finds bring it satisfaction and back to life. The meaning of the phrase is turned on end when we take it as a whole.

And this is a perfect example of how curiosity works. One might face unpleasantness when trying to scratch that curious itch, but the knowledge that comes with the investigation helps us change and grow and understand the universe just a little better.

Indulge in magic that makes you feel good, inside and out.

This is as true for mundane matters as it is for metaphysical ones. You should approach your practice with a curious and open mind. The world is vast and has many things to teach us, if we are just willing to learn.

You need to make sure you are taking precautions when indulging in your curiosity, and we'll discuss those below. As long as you take those precautions, however, you should feel free to explore and play with your magic. Try new, unexpected things. Go to your pantry list and try different herbal combinations in your magic to see how they work. Swap out materia magica, or cast spells at different times to see what happens.

Magic, while it often portrayed as "serious business," can be joyful and fun. You can channel your inner child when you cast magic. Think back to when you were a kid, making potions from water, leaves, and berries in a pot outdoors. Dance in the rain as you collect water for spells. Sing to your plants. Include a sense of wonder and delight in your spellcasting and see if it doesn't raise your spirits.

Indulge in magic that makes you feel good, inside and out. Don't fall into the trap of "shoulds": you should do this kind of magic, you shouldn't engage in that type. If you come away with anything from *A Witch Is*, I hope it is the knowledge that magic is personal. The way you practice it is the perfect way for you.

Childlike curiosity can help guide where you want to focus when it comes to your path as well. Who we were when we were children gives a clear picture of where our interests lay before they were altered and suppressed by society's expectations. Those emotions we felt when we were engaged in "magic" can guide us to what magic feels like when it is successful.

It can be difficult for some to get in touch with those feelings, especially if they had an unsupportive or difficult childhood. Engaging in shadow work can help with working past the negative feelings called up when remembering your childhood experiences. You can start to build a new sense of wonder through prompts such as these:

- When was a time I felt a sense of enchantment?
- What was something from my childhood that felt magical?
- When was a time I was curious about something and indulged that curiosity? What did I learn from the experience?
- What was my childhood dream? How is it still relevant to me today?

As long as you are respectful of yourself and others, use your curiosity to explore magic to your heart's content. Ask questions, but be understanding if not all witches, spirits, or other entities are completely forthcoming.

Safety

We must discuss safety when talking about curiosity. There is a tendency to rush into witchcraft full steam ahead, especially when you are first starting out. We want to know all the things, collect all the materia magica, contact all the spirits, go to the graveyard or crossroads at midnight, and drink deeply from the chalice of magic. And I get it. Learning magic is exciting. Doing our first spell and seeing results inspires us to cast another and then another.

But witches need to take into account a few safety guidelines as they work their magic. These involve avoiding burnout, maintaining protection, and proceeding with caution, especially in areas one isn't familiar with.

Burnout

Burnout can look like not having the energy to work magic. It can be making excuses for not going on a foraging walk or doing your meditation work. It can even manifest as resentment or dread of casting a spell. Listen to your body and emotions, and if you find yourself avoiding doing magic or magic-adjacent activities, it could be a sign that you are reaching a point of exhaustion.

We may be witches, but we are also human beings, and we need to give ourselves grace. Otherwise, we'll find it has been months since we cast a spell and our altar is covered in a thick layer of dust. Burnout can happen for many reasons, the main two being a sense of being overwhelmed and not giving oneself adequate time to rest.

Feeling overwhelmed in our practice can be caused by a variety of triggers. We can have feelings of inadequacy because we feel we don't know enough. This can lead to refusing to work our magic until we know everything about a particular topic. Social media can lead to overwhelm, as it offers up picture-perfect views of others' practices. All those lovely images of cauldrons and herb bundles and artfully arranged altars can quickly go from being inspirational to feeling like indictments of our own witchy failings.

Similarly, perfectionism can keep us from practicing our craft. We want so much for our spells to go off perfectly, so we focus on the details: planning and arranging, shopping for the exact right crystal, and researching the proper shade of green for our candle. We get so caught up on the ideal that we never get around to actually casting the spell.

And then there is the problem of not giving ourselves proper recovery time. This is when you have filled your magical calendar to the brim. You have sabbat and esbat celebrations. You are casting spells on the waxing, full, waning, and new moons in rapid succession. Maybe you have tarot, dream, and spell journals as well as trying to keep a book of shadows. We might feel like we have to make every action magical in order to be a witch. This attitude can lead to burnout in a big way, however.

So how do you address burnout? It depends on what is causing it. This is where you need to get introspective and turn your curiosity on yourself. Journal or use your chosen divination method to get to the root cause of your stress. Ask yourself what is causing the most stress and anxiety when it comes to your magical practice. Or look at what used to energize you and ask why it no longer works. Look at your habits and try to pinpoint where your enthusiasm for witchcraft has gone off the rails.

If the cause is a feeling of inadequacy stemming from not knowing everything, the solution is to remember that you can't know it all. This is something I suffer from often. It ties into imposter syndrome and confidence, as I feel I can't talk on something that I haven't researched extensively. However, the truth of the matter is that even if I had nothing else to occupy my time, I couldn't read all the books, watch all the videos, and visit all the websites on a particular topic. This is where the phrase "unscientific deep dive" can come in handy. It is an idea that you are researching as well as you are able to, using as much time and energy as you can dedicate to what you want to learn. It is a phrase that gives you grace. Don't try to be an expert, but instead be "passionately curious." This shift in attitude should help you overcome the need to know everything before doing.

When it comes to social media–induced burnout, it helps to remember that what you are seeing represents hours of setup and editing by the people who make the posts. What you don't see is the behind-the-scenes work. And so what looks like effortless witchcraft is simply a glamour created by good lighting and editing software. Let that realization help you consume witchy social media more mindfully. When that green-eyed monster of jealousy pops up to compare your practice to others, remember that your witchcraft is unique. No one lives magically in quite the same way as you do. So feeling bad if your practice doesn't match what you are seeing on social media is a pointless waste of energy.

Similarly, if your burnout is due to perfectionism, a change in outlook can help. "Perfect is the enemy of good" is the lesson to take to heart. Put a time limit on the planning stage if you have to. Don't spend more than thirty minutes looking up timings and spell components. Don't stress yourself over rhyming couplets. And don't worry if the moon and stars are in the wrong position for your spellwork. Working a good-enough spell is always superior to a perfect spell that is never cast.

If you find you have been burning the spell candle at both ends, it is time to engage in self-care. This can look like taking bubble baths and binge-watching your favorite comfort show. But it should also look like setting personal boundaries. You may need to curate your time more effectively. Focus on celebrations and events that are personally meaningful to you rather than every witchy holiday that comes up. Your practice isn't less meaningful or valid if you don't celebrate the Wheel of the Year. You can skip full moon observances if they just don't fit into your schedule. And you aren't less of a witch if Halloween just isn't your thing. This requires you taking time to know yourself so that you can be the best witch you can be.

You also need to practice saying no, to others and to yourself. If you find that you are working spells or reading fortunes for everyone who asks, check in with yourself to make sure you are okay with all that expended energy. Not everything has to be magical, and you can sometimes just drink your coffee in the morning rather than stirring in affirmations. One way to keep from burning yourself out at the cauldron is to know when you can take a break from it. This is not an easy task. Especially if you are new to witchcraft and want to do all the things. But build in breaks from magic. Pick days off when you won't do any spellwork. As with any aspect of our life, we need to find moderation so that we're still being our witchy selves years down the road.

Maintaining Protection

Another part of magical safety is maintaining your personal protections. This gets overlooked by new and established witches alike, for different reasons. In the case of newbies, they can forget to lay down protective circles and energies in their rush to get to the meat of a ritual or spell. More experienced witches might neglect their protective routines due to a sense of invulnerability or seeing the practice as a waste of time. Both attitudes open witches up to danger, especially if they work more advanced magic.

What is your protective protocol? Do you set out a magic circle? Do you carry apotropaic charms? Do you cast protective spells on your person and home? If you don't have an answer to these questions, now is the time to think about them. As a witch, you deal with various energies day and night. Not all of them are going to be positive or neutral; some will be actively harmful to you. You need to have a routine way to protect yourself. It should be a method you are so proficient at that it is second nature to you.

Choose a protective measure that makes sense for you. A charm or a piece of jewelry you can charge with protective energies is a good choice if you like physical representations of magic. Psychic and energetic barriers are great if you can't be overt about your witchcraft. Casting a circle before you engage in ritual or spellcasting ensures that no unwelcome energies interfere. But none of these will be helpful if you don't maintain them. Figure out how often you'll need to recharge your charm or recast your protective barrier. If you need to, add an event or reminder to your calendar. Consult a magical timetable to find the best times to do so.

Proceeding with Caution

Related to protective measures is knowing when to proceed with caution. Remember, curiosity killed the cat. The first part of the phrase speaks to the dangers of looking into magical matters. New witches are more likely to take risks that more experienced witches know better to avoid. This is where that curiosity and unscientific deep-dive come in. Before attempting a new bit of magic, especially any dealing with spirits or deities, it is best to spend a little bit of time researching the topic. Find out what others have to say about the spirits or places you are going to work with. There may be guideposts and advice that can make the work easier. Don't fall into the burnout trap of feeling like you have to know everything, but do your research. Get at least three sources of information on the topic. These can be books, videos, blog posts, or even some social media. Revisit the "Vet Your Sources" section on page 144 to refresh yourself on how to evaluate where your information is coming from.

And if you are going to be working with spirits, make sure you know what precautions to take before approaching them. Spirits are just as multifaceted as people. Some are kind and good-natured. Others, however, might be tricksters or even downright mean. No matter the nature of the spirit, you need to protect yourself when dealing with them. This includes not only protection from harm but also knowing how to address the particular spirit, what offerings (if any) they may prefer, what they are willing to help with, and so on.

Caution when approaching and working with other witches is something you should keep in mind as well. Humans, for the most part, are social creatures. When you are first starting out in the practice of witchcraft, you might find yourself trusting implicitly people you've just met because they also claim to be witches. But, just as you vet your sources when it comes to media, you should be doing the same when it comes to the people you meet. You should trust your intuition when it comes to new acquaintances. Do they share your same values? Do they seem to want to engage in genuine sharing of information and wisdom, or do they immediately take on the air of an expert, put down your own thoughts and beliefs, or try to bully you into thinking the way they do? Just because someone says they are magical does not mean they have your best interests at heart. For myself, there are people who, when I meet them, give off a feeling of prickliness, which is my intuition's way of letting me know that we are not likely to get along. In those cases, there have always been problems with butting heads over belief systems, arguments, and a general mutual dislike that develops. I've learned to trust that sense that comes up and take anything these "prickly" people have to say with a grain of salt.

All this is to say that by being certain of your values, such as having a personal mission statement that you created on page 180, will help you know when someone is not the best teacher or co-witch for you. Check in with yourself often, about how it feels when someone says something that is at odds or doesn't align with your beliefs. This may be an opportunity for growth, or it might be something that has no place in your practice. Be careful, also, with being completely open, at least at first, with new acquaintances. You don't have to share everything all at once, and there may be some parts of your practice that you want to keep to yourself. There is no rule that states you have to be an open book to strangers. This is especially true in a day and age when Christian nationalism is on the rise and with regard to the internet. Remember, sometimes not being entirely truthful is essential to your safety.

Taking the time to learn this before you engage shows respect and avoids unnecessary conflict. Be smart and safe in your witchcraft.

Build Your Own Cabinet of Curiosities

Being a witch is very much like being a crow. We tend to collect shiny things, where the definition of *shiny* varies from witch to witch. Right now, on my altar, I have a piece of quartz in the shape of a heart, another stone in the shape of a turtle, a piece of sagebrush wood, a wasp's nest, the body of a bumblebee, a claw from my cat (found on the floor), and a number of other natural oddities. On the windowsill in my kitchen, there is another collection of quartz that I've found on my foraging trips that sits alongside other bits of shiny flotsam, such as marbles and a small plastic duck, that I have found when walking. I keep these items for various reasons. Some of the items lend their energies to my altar and magic; some, like the wasp's nest, are used as materia magica. When I look at each object, I feel a connection to nature and to my own curiosity.

Cabinets of curiosity began to make an appearance in the fifteenth century. Despite being named cabinets, some could take up entire rooms. These collections were often of natural objects that were abnormally shaped or from "foreign" areas and included items like narwhal tusks that were labeled as unicorn horns, insects encased in amber, fossils, corals, and animal specimens. The collections served as the first natural history exhibits, with some even ending up in museums. People continue to create their own curiosity cabinets to this day. For the witch, they can serve either as decor and a piece for conversation or as an altar on which to gather pieces that are filled with energies you can use for your magic.

You can be deliberate when you are filling your cabinet, choosing a theme or type of object that you will collect, or you can be more free-spirited, adding to it a variety of items that speak to you. The point is to fill it with objects that appeal to your witchy side. Choose a place to display your objects, somewhere where you will see them daily. This can be a shadow box, your altar, a windowsill, or whatever space you have available.

Don't feel that you need to be limited to objects, however. You can make a curiosity board, filling a corkboard with photos, pictures, and artwork that represent your interests. Or if you are more artistically inclined, you can keep a sketchbook where you record various items of interest.

Keep the collection dusted and clean and interact with it on a regular basis. Curate your collection, changing out items often so that it is a living testament to your practice.

~~~~~~

As we've seen, curiosity is a powerful tool for witches. It pushes us to pull back the curtain of the mundane and "normal" world to reveal the magic behind it all. Curiosity can be a double-edged sword, however, encouraging us to go beyond the status quo but leading to burnout and fatigue if we indulge in it too often. There needs to be a balance between our passionate curiosity and self-care. One thing you can do is to engage in list making, writing down what you are curious about, so that you can investigate it at a time when you have the means and energy to do so. We will cover a curiosity list next in the exercises section.

 EXERCISES 

Our curiosity taps into various other of our witchy traits. It engages our creativity, our knowledge, and even our kindness. When we look at others, situations, our environment, and our own magic, using our sense of curiosity to look deeper allows us to find the magic in the mundane. To that end, the following exercises are meant to get you used to using your curiosity to seek answers.

The Curiosity List

YOU'LL NEED:

- Your book of shadows (if you keep one), a few sheets of paper, or even the Notes app on your phone
- Something to write with
~~~~~~

As you might have realized by now, I'm a big fan of lists and journaling in my practice. The written word has always played a large part in my life. And so this exercise makes use of writing as a way to get to the heart of your practice.

Start by writing down things you don't know about when it comes to your practice. Perhaps you don't know much about herbs or sigil writing or astrology. Write down whatever comes to mind, without editing or judgment. Write for about five minutes or so or until you have three to five topics. You can, of course, continue writing until you have listed everything that you can come up with.

Go through the list and mark out those topics that pique your interest. Transfer them to a list of topics that you will explore and learn more about. You can set this up as a to-do list, working through each entry one by one. Remember the lessons from the "Vet Your Sources" section on page 144. As you continue on your path, add to your curiosity list other topics that come up. The list will be an ever-growing, ever-changing document to your growth as a witch.

The Failure List

YOU'LL NEED:

- Your book of shadows (if you keep one), a few sheets of paper, or even the Notes app on your phone
- Something to write with

Sometimes magic fails. We can make all the plans, perform all the right steps, use the correct materia magica, and time the spell right, and yet our goals remain frustratingly out of reach. To quote Captain Jean-Luc Picard, "It is possible to commit no mistakes and still lose. That is not a weakness; that is life."[21] And sometimes we just have to take our lumps. But that doesn't mean we can't learn from them.

As an example, I once was trying to get a piece of mail to hurry and get to me. I cast a spell to pull it toward me, envisioning all the hands it needed to go through to make it to my mailbox. I set up the spell with all sorts of materia magica to ease the way, set a realistic deadline for the spell to work, and had honed my visualization and intention to razor-sharp points. And yet, the mail didn't reach me until three days after my deadline. Looking at the postmark, it should have reached me in plenty of time, but when I looked at my spell with a critical and curious eye, I realized that attempting to cast a spell on the United States Postal Service was like trying to hold back the tide. My magic got the piece of mail through the hands of individual people, but that organization was too large for me to influence.

This exercise asks you to look at your magical failures and to interrogate them on why they didn't perform as you wanted them to. This includes spells that just didn't deliver results as well as those that returned results that were different from what you had wanted. You'll need to get comfortable with the idea of failure, not as a fault of your own but as a lesson to learn from.

Write down a spell that failed. Write down everything you did, from the spell itself, to what it was supposed to accomplish, to how you felt about it when you were casting the spell, to what steps you took to mundanely support it. Be as specific as you can.

Next, consider why the spell might have failed. Don't let feelings of disappointment or failure bog you down. Remember, this

21. *Star Trek: The Next Generation*, season 2, episode 21, "Peak Performance," written by David Kemper, directed by Robert Scheerer, aired June 10, 1989.

is a learning experience. Look at it from a lens of curiosity and wonderment. You are just curious about what happened. You can engage in divination, if you want, to help you with this, but often it can be just enough to take a step back and look at the spell in the context of the larger world around you.

So, taking into account what it is that you were doing, consider all the ways or reasons the spell might have gone wrong. If the spell delivered a different result than what you were aiming for, ask yourself why. What could you have done differently to get the results you wanted? What forces might have been working against you? What forces might you have better utilized to see success?

Write down your thoughts on the matter. The point of the exercise isn't so much to help you troubleshoot your spellcasting, although that is a helpful skill to cultivate. It is to get you into a frame of mind where your first reaction to failure is not despair but curiosity.

A Witch Is Confident

You would think that, after having written four books on witchcraft, crafting, and the mashup of the two, I wouldn't suffer from self-doubt any longer. And yet, I am plagued by worries that I'm not witchy enough all the time. It often seems that the more I learn, the more I realize how little I know. Instead of letting that get to me or undermine my self-confidence, however, I try to look at it with excitement.

Being confident in yourself and your abilities can strengthen your magic. You speak with authority and imbue your magic with purpose and direction. When you struggle with self-confidence, your magic has a harder time returning results. Self-confidence also aids you in your relationships, which is very important when it comes to magic. You want to approach any spirits or deities you work with with assurance.

It is easy to lose confidence when it comes to magic. One failed spell and we can start questioning ourselves. This is a natural reaction and one that everyone goes through. Confidence, however, allows us to get back on the broomstick when our magic fails. It gives us greater resilience and belief in our ability to meet obstacles head-on.

There are plenty of reasons why we might lack self-confidence when it comes to our magic. Issues like imposter syndrome and conditions like ADHD can interfere with our certainty in our abilities. But there are many ways to address these challenges. We can summon servitors (something we'll cover in this chapter), create a vision of our ideal self, rely on herbs and crystals and add their energies to boost our confidence, and even use our self-confidence to boost our magic.

Lacking self-confidence is only an obstacle to our practice if we let it be that. If we instead focus on what we know, what we have done in the past, and what we know we can do in the future, our confidence levels will fuel our magic and our practice.

Imposter Syndrome

What do we do when we feel like we're just faking being a witch? When it feels like we're going through the motions, without really dedicating ourselves to the action? How do we combat feelings of inadequacy when we see the curated social media of witches who seem to have it all together? How do we, in short, deal with imposter syndrome? We start by remembering that we're 100 percent that witch.

Then we get off social media. The internet can be a wonderful place and provide so much support and information, but we can take the edited photos, tweets, and videos too seriously. Taking a break from or limiting how much social media you consume can definitely help you deal with imposter syndrome. It also helps to remind yourself that much of what is posted to the internet didn't come easily to the authors. Sometimes hours of work will go into one video or photograph. Captions are often written in a way that caters to the algorithm to get it in front of as many eyes as possible. I'm not implying that it is fake, or that there isn't genuine intent behind those posts. I'm simply pointing out that it is unfair to compare your life to anyone else's, especially if you are comparing yourself to something that has gone through a filter.

Another helpful tool is affirmations. You need to be able to hype yourself up, and affirmations can give you that ability. Choose affirmations that speak directly to what you are feeling negatively about. If you feel like you don't know enough to work magic, tell yourself that "I am always learning and growing my understanding of magic." If you feel like you don't engage in enough witchy stuff to qualify as one, tell yourself, "I am a magical being." The point of affirmations is to counteract the negative self-talk that we engage in when we feel like imposters.

If neither of the above helps, that's when we get magical.

A Servitor for Negative Thoughts

If you have issues with negative self-talk that is getting in the way of you living your most magical life, you might consider creating a servitor to deal with it. A servitor is an autonomous spirit created by a witch to serve a magical task. The concept is one that is frequently used in chaos magic. I have, in the past, used a servitor to help me with my negative thoughts and self-limiting beliefs. And if you find yourself dealing with the same, a servitor might be the right tool for you.

Start with imagining what your servitor will look like. Mine took the form of a raven that I named Nevermore. You can create your servitor in whatever image you prefer: an animal, a person, a ball of light. The image should be one that is pleasant to you, as this servitor will be connected to you for the following months, up to a year. Once you have decided on what it will look like, you are ready to create it.

Since you create and maintain your servitor through your own energy, you'll need to decide how often you will "feed" it. For a servitor to help you with your negative thoughts, you want to feed it energy at least once a month. Set a time, using reminders on your phone if you need to, so that you can feed it on the schedule you set up.

You really want to create as clear a vision as possible.

Finally, you need to figure out how your servitor will help you with your negative thoughts. I envisioned my negative thoughts as gnats and flies that would buzz around my head. So when they would pop up, Nevermore would swoop into action and eat them. You also need to figure out how your negative thoughts manifest. Is it a feeling in your body? Or do you experience a sense of shame or unhappiness? Maybe your body reacts by hunching your shoulders or clenching your hands into fists. However you react, you can then decide how your servitor is going to deal with that. If you feel tightness in your chest, perhaps your servitor places a calming hand there to ease it away. Or if your skin crawls, you might envision your servitor pulling insects off you and disposing of them. You really want to create as clear a vision as possible of both the cause and the reaction.

With all that planning out of the way, you are now ready to create your servitor. You can do this in your astral residence or in mundane space. You will need a purple or silver candle, sandalwood incense, and a piece of quartz crystal. Carve the name of your servitor or just the word *servitor* into your candle. Light the incense and ground and center. Visualize a ball of white light in the center of your chest. Feel it swirling and warming your body.

This is the energy that you will pull from in order to create your servitor.

Light the candle and visualize what your servitor will look like. As you do so, call it by name and give it its task. For example, state, "[Name of servitor], you will remove my negative thoughts when they arise." As you do so, envision pulling a bit of the white light from your chest into the air before you. See your servitor created from that white light. Visualize it taking form in front of you until it is clear as day, surrounded by the white light. Take a little bit of the white light from around the servitor and anchor it into the quartz crystal. This is where the servitor will live when it is not fulfilling its purpose. You can leave the crystal on your altar or carry it around with you.

Let the servitor fade from view. Know that it will keep you company as you go about your daily life. Whenever your negative thoughts arise, picture your servitor taking care of them. When the scheduled time comes to feed the servitor, take a little of the white energy from the center of your chest and add it to the servitor. This will keep the servitor from fading away.

Over time, you might find that you need the servitor less and less. When you recognize your negative thoughts and do something about them, they tend to stop coming up. When and if that happens, you can dismantle your servitor. To do so, envision your servitor and thank it for its service. Explain that it has fulfilled its purpose and is no longer needed in this way. Detach the link between it and the quartz crystal. Then pull the servitor into your chest, returning it to the energy swirling there.

ADHD and Other Conditions

If you are a neurodivergent witch, much of magic can feel out of reach. Things like working with the moon phases or casting circles before you work a spell can feel like they take too much brain power to accomplish. There are so many witches who insist that their way of working magic is the only right way that it can eat away at your confidence in your practice. Let me assure you that how you practice magic is right for you and that's all that matters.

I have lived for years with depression and anxiety. For a while, both interfered in my practice to the point that years passed before I could feel like working magic. During those years, I would feel like a failure as a witch every time I realized I hadn't consulted my tarot deck in months or had watched yet another sabbat pass by without doing anything to honor it. I still have days when I feel like I must be doing something wrong when I can't muster the energy to set out my jar for moon water or when I see that my altar has a layer of dust on it. And as someone who has recently been diagnosed with ADHD, I find the label helps in explaining why I do the things I do, but that often is a small comfort when I continue to struggle in my practice.

This is where I find that working with my conditions, instead of forcing myself to live up to the expectations of someone without them, helps. Taking breaks without giving myself grief over them, resting when I need to, and working with my energy when it is ready has given me a better practice than all those years when I strived for picture-perfect witchcraft. Working with one's conditions will look different from person to person. But the following tips should help you at least find what works best for you.

Rest When Necessary

In our go, go, go world, it is hard to justify taking rest. Naps, so essential to the health and well-being of babies and children, are treated as unnecessary once we become adults. And yet, one in three adults in the United States isn't getting enough sleep.[22] That's a lot of people not getting the rest they need.

When it comes to taking rest, you may just have to tell yourself that you need it and let go of any shame that might be attached to doing so. Of course, if it was as easy as that, there would be no need for writing about it. Instead, it might be better to reframe our associations with sleep and rest. Much like with eating, sleep fuels our body. Without it, we cannot function as well and might even suffer serious consequences. So first, let's acknowledge that we need sleep.

Engage in rest whenever you need it. Make your bed a safe and comfortable place where you can rest easily. Nap when you can. Even a fifteen minute snooze can help you recover and return to the waking world refreshed. If necessary, view your rest as just another tool for working magic. Write down the dreams that come to you when you sleep, or drink some mugwort tea before going to bed in order to encourage prophetic dreams.

Work When You Have the Energy

This was the hardest lesson I ever learned when it came to working my magic while dealing with my various conditions. However, I found that once I started listening to my body instead of my clock, I got more accomplished both magically and mundanely. I was more likely to get stuff done that I had put off for days or weeks. But I had to be okay with the idea that I might not know when I would feel able to do those things that I wanted to do. It meant that my tasks were done in fits and starts. But it also meant I was no longer dragging my feet or resenting what I had to do.

22. "The State of Sleep Health in America 2023," American Sleep Apnea Association, accessed November 21, 2024, https://www.sleephealth.org/sleep-health/the-state-of-sleephealth-in-america/.

Witchcraft often puts a lot of emphasis on magical timing, and so we can feel like if we miss out on a full moon or don't do a communication spell on Wednesday, we have missed the window of opportunity. We forget that magical timing is an aid, not the end-all, be-all for a spell. Our prosperity spell won't fail because we performed it on the waning moon instead of the waxing. So don't get caught up in the idea that you have to work on a time schedule that doesn't work for you.

Give Yourself Grace

At the end of the day, what you have accomplished or not is up to so many factors beyond your control. If you have chronic pain, you might have not had the spoons to do more than just rest. Or you might have had a manic day in which you processed all the herbs that have been drying on the rack for weeks, made incense, cleaned your altar, and started a simmer pot to fill your home with abundant energy. Whatever you manage to do is just right for you at that moment. This is where you give yourself grace and permission to be only as productive as you can reasonably be without doing harm to yourself. Instead of focusing on what you didn't do, list all the things that you did. And if the only thing you can list is that you survived another day, that's a win in any book.

Look into magic you can do that doesn't require as much from you. Sound cleanse rather than relying on smoke bundles if you can't abide the smell of burning things. Light a candle instead of engaging in a full moon ritual. Listen to a podcast or read a book about witchcraft. Journal, doodle, or record a voice note about some magical topic you are interested in. Remember, magic and witchcraft are fueled by intent—that's the only tool you need to engage in your craft.

Using Your Magic to Build Self-Confidence

It may seem, by now, that I suggest magical responses to all life's obstacles. While I don't think magic can solve all our problems, I do think that adding a magical approach to life helps give it a richer context. There's no harm in uttering an affirmation or burning a candle to supplement our mundane means of problem-solving. You can add herbs like peppermint, cinnamon, and ginger to your life to help promote self-assurance and confidence. Burn them as incense or add them to your food while focusing on the energies they bring to you. Carry rose quartz, amazonite, or jasper with you to help boost your self-confidence. You might even go so far as to enchant a piece of jewelry with self-confidence and wear it. Every time you are aware of the jewelry, you will be reminded that you have the confidence inside yourself.

Two other ways to build your self-confidence through magic are to enchant your life and to build an image of the kind of witch you want to be. They both rely on creative magic. You are building a space in which to foster your magical sense of self. And then you create that ideal magical self to embody. Through this magic, you eventually will grow into the witch you long to be, having confidence in your abilities and your path.

Enchant Your Life

When I suggest building your self-confidence by enchanting your life, what I mean is filling your life so full of magic that you feel witchy at all times, no matter what the circumstances.

Play music that makes you feel magical. Music can have a profound impact on our mood, and a well-curated playlist can make all the difference in how you feel. I have several different playlists based on what kind of mood I want to be in. You can use apps like Spotify, Pandora, or YouTube Music to seed a playlist with a couple of songs and then see what the apps recommend to complement them. Create a playlist for when you want to feel magical, when you want to be perked up, and when you need to feel comforted. Play them often, changing in and out songs as you need to until you have the perfect playlist. If you listen often enough, you'll get to the point where hearing just a few chords from a song will switch your mood.

Dressing how you want to feel can help you feel like a witch as well. Clothing not only signals to others how we feel about ourselves, but it can have a profound effect on our state of mind. Take time to build an outfit, or even an entire wardrobe, that helps you get into a magical mindset. This can be kept for only when you cast a spell, or you can wear it out and about, putting off witchy vibes to anyone you encounter. And don't forget the power of accessories. Whenever I feel blah, I know that if I put on my rings and bracelets, I will instantly feel not only more put-together but also more powerful.

Set the tone of your life. Decorate your space in a way that feels uplifting and that reminds you of the magic of life. Burn candles and use aromatherapy to enhance the mood of your home. Make an effort to change out the items on your altar or in your magical workspace to reflect the seasons. Find ways to add magic to the mundane chores of your life. Turn sweeping or vacuuming into a cleansing ritual. Add moon water to your dishwashing so that the dishes are also blessed as well as cleaned. Place crystals or spell pouches around your space to help protect it. All that is required of you is to put in the effort to think differently about what you do and how you do it.

Enchanting your life takes nothing more than your creative effort. It means looking at your life through a magical lens. By doing so, you are wrapping yourself up in a cocoon of enchantment. The more magical you feel, the more self-confidence you'll have.

Being the Witch You Want in Your Life

You can make use of your astral residence to build your self-confidence in much the same way that you used it to integrate your shadow self on page 117. In that case, you incorporated a visualization of your shadow self into your body. This time you will do the same with a visualization of your confident self.

Enter your astral residence in the way you normally would, whether this is through the stairway method or another way. Once you have entered, make yourself comfortable and take a few deep breaths. Center and ground yourself, and then start building an image of what your ideal self looks like. What does this person wear? Do they have the same haircut and color as you do, or is it different? What is their style? Now move your focus away from the outward appearance and on to how this person acts, thinks, and feels. You can add in characteristics that you'd like to embody, as well as how you would want to live your life. Spend more time on the interior aspects of this ideal self, as you will be more likely to embody them as you incorporate it into your life.

Treat your vision like it is a suit that you can just put on.

Once you have created a vision of this ideal self, it's time to merge it with you. Walk over to the vision and enter it. Treat your vision like it is a suit that you can just put on. See it settle into your body, just under your skin. Move around and experience what it would be like to be this ideal self. Think of a situation in the past when you felt flustered or upset. How would you handle it now as the best, most magical version of yourself? Imagine a scenario in which you failed at something. What would your ideal self have done differently? This kind of role-play gives you the opportunity to try out the image you created to make sure that it is what you want. It also gives you practice in being this self.

When you are done, you can leave your astral residence, carrying your ideal self with you into the mundane world. Repeat this exercise whenever you feel like you aren't being true to your witchy self or ideals.

Using Your Self-Confidence to Boost Your Magic

Maybe the issue isn't that you lack self-confidence but that you aren't sure about your magical abilities. This can happen, especially when you start out. It can be a leap of faith to go from being assured in your mundane life to trusting in your magical practice. To that end, you might need to remind yourself that your skills and beliefs are valid and useful whether you are fixing a problem with your budget or fixing a problem in your love life.

When you are confident in your day-to-day life, that poise carries over to your magical practice. Affirmations can help in this instance. When you are feeling unsure about your abilities, you can remind yourself that "I am magical" or "My magic is powerful and sees results."

Lifelong Magical Learning

There is always something new to learn. This is especially true when it comes to magic, as there are thousands of years of knowledge and experience in the historical record. That can be daunting at any time for beginner and experienced witches alike. It can be easy to feel like we aren't knowledgeable enough when new information pops up all the time, especially if that information contradicts what we believe or thought we knew. The key to dealing with this upset is to remember that witches are lifelong learners.

Read broadly. If reading isn't your thing, there are audiobooks, podcasts, and videos that cover a range of witchy topics. Make sure to expose yourself to voices that you might not usually entertain. This might mean finding witches of color, witches from minority or marginalized groups, and witches whose beliefs might not neatly align with your own. Listen to witches who are both older and younger than yourself. This is useful in keeping your views from becoming calcified and inflexible.

Don't forget to seek out knowledge from beings other than humans as well. Go into nature, talk to the spirits, and call on deities and ancestors to aid you in your learning. They can give you perspectives you wouldn't get from humans. Nature informs us that the universe moves in cycles, as should we. Spirits have lessons about the land that can aid us in our magic. Deities and ancestors can give you access to long-forgotten knowledge. All of this can help you refine and focus your understanding of your own magical practice.

Finally, listen to yourself. Your body and mind can tell you so much about how magic affects you personally, from how you best raise energy to what your body needs to recover from spellworking. The more in tune you are with yourself, the more effective your magic will be because you've made it personal.

~~~

Confidence is one of those qualities that is hard to build and easy to lose. But if you focus on the fact that you are a witch and that you can work magic, that is a majority of the hard work done. If
~~~

you avoid comparing yourself to others and remember that magic is personal, meaning that you should be working with your own lifestyle, strengths, and weaknesses, that's the rest of the equation.

 EXERCISES 

Building self-confidence can be a difficult task, especially if you haven't had much cause to believe in yourself. The following exercises are designed to help you become more self-assured in your practice. Even if you don't find yourself lacking in that category, it is good to go through the exercises.

Your Confidence List

You'll need:

- Your book of shadows (if you keep one), a few sheets of paper, or even the Notes app on your phone
- Something to write with

Sometimes you just need to make a list of the things you are confident about. That's exactly what you will be doing in this exercise. You are going to write down three things that you are confident doing as a witch. You are not limited to three; this is just the minimum that you need to list.

You can focus on spells, research, types of magic, or other activities, as long as they are in service to your witchy path. Write down not only what the activity is but why you are confident that you can do it. Maybe you work with a local spirit or a deity on a regular basis, and you know that if you called on them, they would answer. Or perhaps you have a well-developed support network of like-minded witches that you know you could call upon for information if you didn't know something. Whatever it is, write it down.

Now, you are going to look at the opposite. What are three things you don't feel confident doing as a witch? These should be activities that you would like to get better at but currently don't feel like you have a good handle on. As with the first list, you aren't limited to just three, but that is the starting point. Also write down why you don't feel confident about your abilities with these things. Maybe you don't feel like you know enough about a topic. Or perhaps you feel you don't have the right materials for a certain kind of spell.

What steps could you take to become more confident in performing the items on this second list? Are there resources or talents from the first list that could help you with the second one? Choose one of the items from the second list to work on. Do whatever you need—research, gathering materials, practicing meditation, working on your intuition—to gain experience doing that activity. Perhaps you have never worked with a deity before and are interested in doing so. Take time to do the research into the deity, build an altar to them, and invoke them according to what you have learned. Set a timeline for doing so.

Once you have done this, you can move that item from the second list to the first. You now have built confidence in a new skill or ability. You can repeat this process as many times as you want, and as you do so, you'll find that your confidence in your practice grows over time.

Looking Over Your Magical Record

YOU'LL NEED:

- Your book of shadows (if you keep one), a few sheets of paper, or even the Notes app on your phone
- Something to write with

By now you should have created some sort of method to track your work on your path. This might be a book of shadows or a journal. It might just be a mark in your planner of times when you have cast a spell. However you keep track of your magical workings, now is the time to go back over it and start highlighting your successes.

Using sticky notes, highlighters, or bookmarks, identify those places where you have enjoyed success in your spellcasting. These don't have to be large or flashy acts of magic. In fact, your most successful spells might have accomplished small, personal goals. Also mark out times when you engaged in magical works like divination, dream interpretation, working with spirits, and the like, when you felt especially witchy.

By highlighting these instances, you are building a success list that you can return to whenever you feel like you are not making headway as a witch. These past successes can encourage you when you hit setbacks. They can also point to where you are strongest. You can look over your past successful work and determine what kind of magic works the best for you. Note things like when you worked the magic, how you were feeling when you did it, and what you used in your spells. You can even transfer these insights into a new page of your book of shadows or journal so that you have them all in one place to refer to in the future.

You can also take note of those times when the magic failed. Try to determine why your spells didn't work. Was it a new type of magic that you didn't have any experience in? Did the spirits not show up when you called? Were the tarot cards giving you unclear answers? By going over what didn't work, you can make sure you don't repeat past mistakes.

Going over the past provides fuel for future fireworks. Whether you succeeded or failed, you still learned something that you can put into practice now. When faced with failures, don't let them get to you, for they can teach you more than success does. As long as you keep your mind open and approach this exercise with curiosity, you will build confidence in your future spellcasting.

Conclusion

I've been a witch all my life. Even before I had a word for it or understood what it would mean, I knew that I was magical. The lessons in *A Witch Is* are hard-won over years of practice and nonpractice. I spent my time in the broom closet and then many years out but not really doing anything about it. But always, at the back of my mind, the ideas of what it meant to be a witch have percolated, bubbling just as surely as the potion in a witch's cauldron. With each new lesson that emerged, I became more confident in my practice and craft. I hope that *A Witch Is* has done the same for you.

Being a witch means being someone who approaches the world from a different perspective. We look for the magic behind the mundane. We see links and connections where others can't. It is that different worldview that separates us from other, nonmagical people more than anything else. I believe that with this mindset comes a responsibility to ourselves to make the most of our magic. These lessons are meant to help you in that regard.

With certain exceptions—relating to closed practices and orders that have initiatory practices—your word is good enough to claim the title *witch*. You don't need someone else, or a book, to know what is in your heart. It is enough that you say you are a witch. There are those who try to gatekeep witchcraft. It will be the confidence and self-awareness that you built that will keep you from listening to those who would exclude you.

To take on that label, however, is to set out on a path that makes a few demands of you. It requires faith and belief in magic and other unseen forces. You are asked to take responsibility for your actions. And magic calls on us to be true to ourselves. The lessons in *A Witch Is* are all in support of those requirements. I have presented them to you in hopes that they will help you develop your craft into a robust system by which you can live a magical life.

If nothing else, I hope *A Witch Is* has challenged you to take a renewed look at your beliefs and practice. Witchcraft isn't a religion, but that doesn't mean that morals and ethics don't apply to it. By the end of this book, you should have a better understanding not only of what witchcraft means to you but of yourself as well.

Acknowledgments

The idea for *A Witch Is* was years in the making. I first considered writing a set of lessons for my daughter, Charlotte, when she turned twelve as a sort of primer for her magical life. Life, as it is wont, got in the way of those plans, so I set them aside. Then, a couple of years ago, I revisited the idea. By then my daughter was long past twelve years old, and I realized that it was a set of lessons more for myself than for her. But no matter who the audience is, this book wouldn't have been born if it were not for her inspiration, so I have to give thanks for her.

I also wouldn't have written this book if it weren't for the encouragement of my editor, Elysia Gallo, to submit another idea to her. I will always be thankful for her guidance of my writing as it grew from an idea to a fully fledged book. I would also like to thank Lauryn Heineman for her thoughtful edits to the book. Between the two of them, *A Witch Is* is stronger for their help. I am also grateful to Llewellyn, which has been so supportive of all my books over the years.

Finally, I'd like to thank my husband, Stephan, for all the support he has given me, especially when I am writing. He takes care of the house and the family so that I can concentrate on my work.

Recommended Reading

Blackthorn's Protection Magic: A Witch's Guide to Mental and Physical Self-Defense by Amy Blackthorn

Psychic Witch: A Metaphysical Guide to Meditation, Magick & Manifestation by Mat Auryn

Protection & Reversal Magick: A Witch's Defense Manual by Jason Miller

Alive with Spirits: The Path and Practice of Animistic Witchcraft by Althaea Sebastiani

Llewellyn's Complete Book of North American Folk Magic: A Landscape of Magic, Mystery, and Tradition edited by Cory Thomas Hutcheson

Bibliography

Auryn, Mat. "Mind Magick" panel. Between the Worlds/Sacred Space Conference. April 7, 2023.

Crowley, Aleister. *Magick in Theory and Practice.* Lecram Press, 1929.

Doran, George T. "There's a S.M.A.R.T. Way to Write Management's Goals and Objectives." *Management Review* 70, no. 11 (1981): 35–36. https://community.mis.temple.edu/mis0855002fall2015/files/2015/10/S.M.A.R.T-Way-Management-Review.pdf.

Einstein, Albert. *The Expanded Quotable Einstein.* Edited by Alice Calaprice. Princeton University Press, 2000.

Herrington, Randy, dir. *Road House.* Silver Pictures, 1989.

McCoy, Edain. *A Witch's Guide to Faery Folk: How to Work with the Elemental World.* Llewellyn, 2002.

MythBusters. Season 10, episode 8, "Bouncing Bullet." Aired May 13, 2012, on Discovery Channel.

Pratchett, Terry. *Lords and Ladies.* Harper Collins, 1996. Kindle.

Star Trek: The Next Generation. Season 2, episode 21, "Peak Performance." Written by David Kemper. Directed by Robert Scheerer. Aired June 10, 1989.

To Write to the Author

If you wish to contact the author or would like more information about this book, please write to the author in care of Llewellyn Worldwide Ltd. and we will forward your request. Both the author and the publisher appreciate hearing from you and learning of your enjoyment of this book and how it has helped you. Llewellyn Worldwide Ltd. cannot guarantee that every letter written to the author can be answered, but all will be forwarded. Please write to:

Raechel Henderson
℅ Llewellyn Worldwide
2143 Wooddale Drive
Woodbury, MN 55125-2989

Please enclose a self-addressed stamped envelope for reply, or $1.00 to cover costs. If outside the U.S.A., enclose an international postal reply coupon.

Many of Llewellyn's authors have websites with additional information and resources. For more information, please visit our website at http://www.llewellyn.com.